T0048621

ALSO BY JOHN BERRYMAN

POETRY

Poems (1942)

The Dispossessed (1948)

Homage to Mistress Bradstreet (1956)

His Thought Made Pockets & The Plane Buckt (1958)

77 Dream Songs (1964)

Berryman's Sonnets (1967)

Short Poems (1967)

Homage to Mistress Bradstreet and Other Poems (1968)

His Toy, His Dream, His Rest (1968)

The Dream Songs (1969)

Love & Fame (1970)

Delusions, Etc. (1972)

Henry's Fate & Other Poems, 1967–1972 (1977)

Collected Poems 1937–1971 (1989)

PROSE

Stephen Crane: A Critical Biography (1950)

The Arts of Reading (with Ralph Ross and Allen Tate) (1960)

Recovery (1973)

The Freedom of the Poet (1976)

Berryman's Shakespeare (1999)

The Heart Is Strange

JOHN BERRYMAN

The Heart Is Strange

NEW SELECTED POEMS

REVISED EDITION

Edited and with an introduction by Daniel Swift

Farrar, Straus and Giroux

New York

Farrar, Straus and Giroux
18 West 18th Street, New York 10011

The Library of Congress has cataloged the hardcover edition as follows:
Berryman, John, 1914–1972.
    [Poems, Selections.]
    The heart is strange : new selected poems / John Berryman ; edited with
an introduction by Daniel Swift. — First edition.
        pages   cm
    ISBN 978-0-374-22108-9 (hardback)
    I. Swift, Daniel, 1977–   II. Title.

PS3503.E744 A6 2014
811'.54—dc23

                                                                    2014004039

                Paperback ISBN: 978-0-374-53578-0

                Designed by Jonathan D. Lippincott

Our books may be purchased in bulk for promotional, educational, or
business use. Please contact your local bookseller or the Macmillan Corporate
and Premium Sales Department at 1-800-221-7945, extension 5442, or
by e-mail at MacmillanSpecialMarkets@macmillan.com.

                        www.fsgbooks.com
        www.twitter.com/fsgbooks • www.facebook.com/fsgbooks

                    1   3   5   7   9   10   8   6   4   2

Contents

Introduction

John Berryman saw birthdays as imaginative opportunities. Lecturing at Princeton in March 1951, he pictured Shakespeare on his thirtieth birthday. "Suppose with me a time, a place, a man who was waked, risen, washed, dressed, fed, congratulated, on a day in latter April long ago," he began: "about April 22, say, of 1594, a Monday." A birthday is a chance to greet across time: to hail a predecessor. In a late poem Berryman addressed Emily Dickinson. It is December 10, 1970, and in "Your Birthday in Wisconsin You Are 140" he raises his glass to her. "Well. Thursday afternoon, I'm in W——," he writes: "drinking your ditties, and (dear) *they* are *alive*." A birthday is a moment of invention. The climax of his long poem "Homage to Mistress Bradstreet" is a violent, beautiful childbirth. "No. No. Yes! everything down / hardens I press with horrible joy down," shouts Anne: "I did it with my body!" Close to the end of *The Dream Songs*, the cycle for which Berryman is best known, he writes: "Tomorrow is his birthday, makes you think." John Berryman was born in McAlester, Oklahoma, on October 25, 1914, and this selection of his poems marks his centenary.

Bringing a man to life: this was his imaginative project. On March 12, 1969, collecting a prize at the National Book Awards, Berryman explained that his aim in *The Dream Songs* was "the reproduction or invention of the motions of a human personality, free and determined." These poems describe a sad man called Henry. "So may be Henry was a human being," he writes in Dream Song 13:

> Let's investigate that.
> . . . We did; okay.
> He is a human American man.

In producing him, they explore the conditions of his invention. "Let us suppose," he begins, in Dream Song 15:

one pal unwinding from his labours in
one bar of Chicago,
and this did actual happen. This was so.

Just because we must imagine him does not mean that he is not real; nor is he exactly the same as Berryman. "The poem," he asserts in a note, "is essentially about an imaginary character (not the poet, not me) named Henry," but the distance between the two remains a little blurred.

Berryman has not been canonized, quite; he has not continued to receive the respect, even awe, accorded to his great contemporaries Robert Lowell and Elizabeth Bishop. This may be because he appears a little less serious than they do. He is certainly funnier than they are, constantly mirthful about the process of critical celebration and literary canonization. "[L]iterature bores me, especially great literature," complains Dream Song 14. "Henry bores me, with his plights & gripes / as bad as achilles," it continues, and the joke is only half that Henry is no Achilles. It is also in the mismatch of classical literature and teenage ennui, balanced by the voice.

Berryman has, however, found a curious afterlife in the early decades of the twenty-first century. He appears unexpectedly and often in songs by indie rock bands. In "Mama, Won't You Keep Them Castles in the Air and Burning?" by the band Clap Your Hands Say Yeah, the singer intones joylessly, "I came softly, slowly / Banging me metal drum / Like Berryman." The Australian singer Nick Cave named one of his albums *Henry's Dream* (1992), and in the song "We Call Upon the Author" from 2008 he returns to Berryman. "Berryman was the best!" he yelps: "He wrote like wet papier-mâché, went the Heming-way."

These bands take Berryman as an emblem of the hard-living, misunderstood poet: it is a Romantic vision of the man and hinges upon his alcoholism, suffering, and early death. Berryman committed suicide by jumping from the Washington Avenue Bridge in Minneapolis in January 1972, and this is the moment these songs return to. "There was that night that we thought John Berryman could fly," sing the band The Hold Steady in "Stuck Between Stations," and the song invents the scene. "The Devil and John Berryman, they took a walk together," the song imagines, and it starts to speak for him: "He said, 'I've sur-rounded myself with doctors and deep thinkers / Their big heads and soft bodies make for lousy lovers.'"

"John Allyn Smith Sails" by the band Okkervil River borrows Berry-man's original name and mixes his story with a classic pop song from the 1960s. The fortuitously named "Sloop John B" is in turn a pop cover of an old folk song, and this new version ends with Berryman's voice:

> I'm full in my heart and my head
> And I want to go home
> With a book in each hand
> In the way I had planned
> Well, I feel so broke up, I want to go home.

"With a book in each hand": this is the final image of the first volume of Dream Songs, 77 *Dream Songs*, as a worn-down Henry determines to keep living:

> with in each hand
> one of his own mad books and all,
> ancient fires for eyes, his head full
> & his heart full, he's making ready to move on.

Outside the confines of his own published works, Berryman's words and image have moved into popular American myth, blended with the Faustian backstory of the blues—a singer who trades with the devil—and the old notion of the artist as troubled outsider. Like the Dream Songs, these indie rock bands are supposing a man, someone halfway between the invented and the real.

These are all, however, versions of Berryman's life, and when we turn to the works they may at first look tied to a particular historical period. Berryman's poems are filled with the bric-a-brac of 1950s and 1960s America: *Ben Hur*, Ike, the Viet Cong, and Buddhist monks setting themselves on fire. We hear of medicines and magazines of the time: LSD, Sparine, Haldol, and Serax; *National Geographic* and *Time*.

His characters eat chicken paprika and drink frozen daiquiris, and speak lines from old vaudeville shows. Berryman loved blues music, and alludes to it throughout: Bessie Smith, Pinetop Perkins, "Empty Bed Blues" ("empty grows every bed" ends the first Dream Song). In "New Year's Eve" from Berryman's first full collection, *The Dispossessed* (1948), the speaker is at a party where "Somebody slapped / Somebody's second wife somewhere," and the line conjures an age perhaps best known to us now from TV shows. It is easy to read these poems as historical documents.

This is, however, too narrow an understanding of Berryman's sense of history: for his listing of all these temporary possessions and fashions is also in the service of an ambition outside time. He wishes to capture what it is to be a human, alive and present in the culture. Reading Berryman therefore involves a little time travel, and this is the magic trick of deeply sympathetic literature: to exist in one instant both in the past and present, in two places at once. *Berryman's Sonnets* trace the story of a love affair, and one of them describes an evening when Berryman and his lover are far from each other. They have agreed to each separately at six o'clock go to a bar. "I lift—lift you five States away your glass," he explains, and although she has never been to this bar— "Wide of this bar you never graced"—and although there are other, ugly sounds and interruptions—"wet strange cars pass" and "The spruce barkeep sports a toupee alas"—they are for this moment with each other. "Grey eyes light! and we have our drink together," it ends. Written before an age of cell phones, this event seems oddly archaic, sweet and old-fashioned. It is also magical, in its faith in will over circumstance, and it is what we do—in miniature—when we read. Berryman invites us to drink with him. In reading his poems, we clink glasses across the decades.

To celebrate Berryman on his one hundredth birthday, Farrar, Straus and Giroux have reissued his three major collections of poetry: *Berryman's Sonnets*, *77 Dream Songs*, and the complete cycle of 385 Dream Songs. Each has a new introduction by a poet: April Bernard, Henri Cole, and Michael Hofmann. In preparing this second edition of the New Selected volume, I have consulted with these three poets in choosing representative samples from both the sonnets and the Dream Songs, and I have tried to include those that show Berryman's skill and style as a poet as well as those that are, simply, our favorites. But these three collections are not all of Berryman's published poetry. This New Selected draws upon the whole of Berryman's career. Here are poems from his first major collection, *The Dispossessed* (1948); the complete "Homage to Mistress Bradstreet" (1953), which is his masterpiece, in the old-fashioned sense of the word—the early work that proves an apprentice is now a master of his chosen form; and from the moving two late collections, *Love & Fame* (1970) and *Delusions, Etc.* (1972). This volume also includes poems from the smaller collections published in Berryman's lifetime, and for these I gratefully follow the texts established by Charles Thornbury in his *John Berryman: Collected Poems 1937–1971* (1989), with the exceptions explained below. Thornbury includes only verse selected and arranged for publication by Berryman personally: he leaves out, for example, the poems written very late in Berryman's life and collected after his death by John Haffenden in *Henry's Fate & Other Poems, 1967–1972* (1977). I have included poems from this volume among the selection in order to give as broad a sample as possible.

In addition to Berryman's poetry published as collections, this New Selected volume includes also a poem by Berryman that has not previously appeared among his published poetry. "Mr. Pou & the Alphabet" was published for the first time in Richard J. Kelley's edition of Berryman's letters to his mother, *We Dream of Honour* (1988), and is addressed to his son, Paul. Paul was born in March 1957, and the following year his second wife, Ann, left him, taking their son with her. Berryman remarried in the fall of 1961, and that Christmas he wrote "Mr. Pou & the Alphabet" for his separated son. It is an alphabet poem. It is tender and playful, but also a little somber. "A is for *awful*, which things are," it begins. "B is for *bear* them, well as we can." This is an older Berryman, one worn down by the world but still enduring, and one who loved his children, who are an important presence in his poetry. The final phrase of the Dream Songs is simply "my heavy daughter," and among his papers at his death was the opening for a new long poem he hoped to write, on his three children and their futures.

Any selection implies an interpretation. Berryman has long been seen—and often dismissed—as a merely "confessional" poet, and while the urge to narrate his own collapses was certainly a motor for him, he is also a poet of many more voices than this. Confession, of course, has a religious origin, and Berryman was a powerful devotional poet. This New Selected includes his two cycles of liturgical verse, "Eleven Addresses to the Lord" and "Opus Dei," in full. While he wrote these late in his career, the devotional impulse runs throughout his works. "What he has now to say is a long / wonder the world can bear & be," he writes in the first Dream Song, and the struggle to make sense of an apparently cruel world is one strand among these astonishingly rich works. I have hoped, in my selection, to show Berryman's development as a poet, which was a movement through styles and forms. This introduction traces some key concerns and motifs through his career.

On January 10, 1938, Berryman wrote to his mother. "The problem of the name has arisen again," he explained, for he had just submitted poems to two little magazines under two different names, John McAlpin Berryman and J.A.M. Berryman. He had already decided to divide his writing life by name—John Berryman for poetry and plays, and J.A.M. Berryman for the rest—so his confusion was understandable. Now he feared it might deter readers. He was twenty-three years old, and planning for wide recognition.

The problem of the name arises only in part from Berryman's great ambition; it is also a wholly sensible response to the deep uncertainty of his family structure. His childhood was a chaos of shifting names and uncertain relations. His mother called him Billy before he was born and until he was three, but he was christened John Allyn Smith, after his father. When his father died in June 1926—a suicide, it seems, although there is haze around even this—his mother soon remarried, this time to the family's landlord, a man called John Angus McAlpin Berryman. It is customary for a woman to change her last name upon marriage, but Berryman's mother changed her first name too. Martha Smith became Jill Angel Berryman and she renamed her son after his new father. The name John Berryman, then, is doubly borrowed, thirdhand. At school his friends nicknamed him Burrman, for he slurred his own name. Later, his first wife recalled him saying, "What I cannot forgive myself for not having done, was to take the name John Smith," and in penance he repeated his actual name like a mantra or a curse.

He liked language that is particular to place. At school in Connecticut as a young teenager he collected slang: "hours," "called up," a "heeler." He reported these to his mother, and when he arrived in England in 1936 he immediately wrote home to explain the local currency: "Sixpence is a tanner, the shilling a bob, the pound a quid." He was on his way to Cambridge University, where he had been awarded a fellowship and where he dressed in tweed suits and changed his voice. He was twenty-one. "I suppose it is correct to say that I prefer their accent to the 'American' accent," he wrote. For the rest of his life he followed English spelling both in private letters and his published work. W. S. Merwin was a student of Berryman's at the University of Iowa in 1946, and he recalled his teacher's voice: "[H]e snapped down his nose with an accent / I think he had affected in England." Just as his voice was a copy, so too were his habits. In March 1937 Dylan Thomas visited Cambridge, and Berryman took up heavy drinking in imitation of the great Welsh alcoholic. In the summer of 1941 he was courting his wife-to-be in New York City, and one night they tried to find a restaurant for dinner. "How much easier it would be if we were abroad," he told her: "Now, if we were in Paris, we could go to La Coupole." He was imagining them as Scott and Zelda Fitzgerald, or himself as Hemingway, figures of another generation.

Reading Berryman's early poetry is like playing a guessing game: who does he sound like now? He is Thomas here, and then he is Yeats; here he is Auden and here he is Eliot. It is by walking through this funhouse of mirrors and influences that he became himself. The very early "Winter Landscape" rewrites Dylan Thomas's "A Refusal to Mourn the Death, by Fire, of a Child in London" as it imagines a "morning occasion"—not "mourning," but the sound is the same, and he is sensitive to sound, this man of accents—and as it pictures

The long companions they can never reach,
The blue light, men with ladders, by the church
The sledge and shadow in the twilit street . . .

This follows Thomas:

Deep with the first dead lies London's daughter,
Robed in the long friends,
The grains beyond age, the dark veins of her mother,
Secret by the unmourning water . . .

"Winter Landscape" was written in January 1939; in February 1940
he began "A Point of Age," which turns oddly in the fourth stanza into
Anglo-Saxon alliterative meter:

Odysseys I examine, bed on a board,
Heartbreak familiar as the heart is strange.

This becomes less unexpected when placed alongside the opening of Ezra
Pound's Canto I, which rewrites a scene from the *Odyssey* in that meter:

And then went down to the ship,
Set keel to breakers, forth on the godly sea, and
We set up mast and sail on that swart ship,
Bore sheep aboard her, and our bodies also
Heavy with weeping . . .

His titles echo others; he is borrowing his syntax and vocabulary; he is
a young man, taking what is good, trying out what works. It is worth
playing this footnote game now, for later, and culminating in *The
Dream Songs*, Berryman will turn mimicry to his advantage and invent
a poetics that is also an echo chamber. He will find a voice that is
recognizably his own—perhaps the most distinctive voice of twentieth-
century American poetry—but he will find it in the voices of others.
To echo him: The heartbreak is familiar but the heart is strange.

In his first full collection, *The Dispossessed* (1948), he is often looking forward and anticipating what is ahead. "At twenty-five a man is on his way," begins "A Point of Age," and here he is fixated by the time of day and the time of life. "There was a kind of fever on the clock / That morning," he writes in "Parting as Descent." As poems about other poets and as poems about coming-of-age these are also, of course, poems about finding a place in the tradition. In "The Possessed" he pictures the dead before him:

This afternoon, discomfortable dead
Drift into doorways, lounge, across the bridge,
Whittling memory at the water's edge,
And watch. This is what you inherited.

The poem follows the poetic vocabulary of T. S. Eliot and also the terms of his famous essay "Tradition and the Individual Talent":

No poet, no artist of any art, has his complete meaning alone. His significance, his appreciation is the appreciation of his relation to the dead poets and artists. You cannot value him alone; you must set him, for contrast and comparison, among the dead.

This is the work of these early poems. Berryman is setting himself among the dead, counting up his inheritance.

There are also innovations, things particularly his, and since we know what Berryman became it is impossible now to read these early poems but with our own sense of anticipation; we know where he is going to get to and we wait for its first occurrence. Here are two early premonitions of the later Berryman. Berryman wrote "The Moon and the Night and the Men" on May 28, 1940, in Detroit. He was waiting for news from his girlfriend, who was in England; he had spent the winter alone in a freezing five-room apartment. This is a strange war poem, taking place at a distance from the war that had broken out six months before but which America would not join for almost another two years. The scene is an army base, somewhere in America, and it begins:

> On the night of the Belgian surrender the moon rose
> Late, a delayed moon, and a violent moon
> For the English or the American beholder;
> The French beholder. It was a cold night,
> People put on their wraps, the troops were cold
> No doubt, despite the calendar, no doubt
> Numbers of refugees coughed, and the sight
> Or sound of some killed others. A cold night.

A new confidence is shown in the handling of syntax, which here is a little twisted in order to open up and double the meanings. The delayed "no doubt" turns an observation of local conditions into a guess about what might be happening far out of sight. And slang here is important: "killing" takes both the demotic sense of making someone laugh and also something wholly more violent.

The second innovation is more striking, more severe. There are nine "Nervous Songs" in *The Dispossessed*, and they follow the same form of three six-line stanzas. Each takes a different voice: jagged, energetic, jumpy. "A Professor's Song" is sung by a dusty, aggressive academic; "The Song of the Demented Priest" describes aging and an incipient loss of faith. "Young Woman's Song" is anxious, taut, with something worried and sexual just beneath the lines. "I hate this something like a bobbing cork / Not going," she says: "I want something to hang to.—" With this short cycle of poems, each in the same stanzaic form as the later Dream Songs, Berryman learned an important lesson: that the poem takes place between the lines. The young woman says, "What I am looking for (*I am*) may be / Happening in the gaps of what I know," and this is true for Berryman's own poetics, discovered through speaking like another.

It is conventional to describe Berryman as "confessional": as one of a group of American poets of the 1950s and 1960s, including also

Robert Lowell and Sylvia Plath, for whom the use of personal material was a special and distinguishing mark. In 1962, the English critic A. Alvarez celebrated what he saw as "a new seriousness" in these poets: "I would define this seriousness simply as the poet's ability and willingness to face the full range of his experience with his full intelligence; not to take the easy exits of either the conventional response or choking incoherence." This poetry would be open to all the experience of modern life, and particularly its grit: it would address suicide, depression, banality. This claim appeared in the introduction to a hugely popular anthology called *The New Poetry*, and Berryman was the first poet in it.

More recently, Adam Kirsch has suggested that our attention to the apparently intimate contents of the works of these poets has distracted us from their careful artifice. "To treat their poems mainly as documents of personal experience is not just to diminish their achievement, but to ignore their unanimous disdain for the idea of confessional poetry," Kirsch writes in *The Wounded Surgeon* (2005):

> Plath scorned the idea of poetry as "some kind of therapeutic public purge or excretion"; Berryman insisted that "the speaker [of a poem] can never be the actual writer," that there is always "an abyss between [the poet's] person and his persona"; Bishop deplored the trend toward "more and more anguish and less and less poetry"; Lowell explained that even in *Life Studies*, usually considered the first masterpiece of confessional poetry, "the whole balance of the poem was something invented."

The tenacity of the term "confessional" lies partly in a way of reading: we feel that the real biographical experience gives the poem weight, and yet this is also, of course, a deliberate literary effect. Particularly in Berryman, there is a careful balance of new freedom and old form. That which is hidden is set against that which is displayed, as if each poem were half a secret.

Berryman was highly sensitive to form. In 1932, William Carlos Williams instructed his generation:

Don't write sonnets. The line is dead, unsuited to the language. Everything that can ever be said from now until doomsday in the sonnet form has been better said in twelfth-century Italian.

Berryman's whole career might be understood as a rebuke to this. In 1934, he wrote his first surviving poems: they are four Shakespearean sonnets, and they celebrate his mother's fortieth birthday. The following year he tried to seduce a Barnard student by writing sonnets for her, and when in February 1947 he began an affair with a married woman he met in Princeton, he turned again to this form. "I wanted a *familiar* form in which to *put* the *new*," he wrote in his journal: "Clearly a sonnet sequence. And this gave me also a wonderful to me sense of continuity with lovers dead."

Her name was Chris. The poems insist upon this: they are little boasts. He describes her blond hair and her clothes, her naked body as she sleeps. "You, Chris, *contrite* I never thought to see," begins one: "Whom nothing fazes, no *crise* can disconcert, / Who calm cross crises all year." He repeats the name in puns: he favors words such as "crisis" and "syncrisis." He lists the days upon which they met—July 3, July 4— and he wishes to invent a new poetic language to express their specific love.

> I prod our English: cough me up a word,
> Slip me an epithet will justify
> My daring fondle . . .

he writes, as if the language itself were complicit in their affair. In sonnet 23 he turns upon the traditional vocabulary and image-set of love poetry:

> Also I fox 'heart', striking a modern breast
> Hollow as a drum, and 'beauty' I taboo;
> I want a verse fresh as a bubble breaks,
> As little false . . .

He is trying to remake the familiar form so that it may hold the new. Yet perhaps the problem is precisely that these sonnets have what Berryman called "a sense of continuity." Like the emotions, these poems are deeply referential: Berryman mentions or alludes to Marlowe, Petrarch, Wyatt, Sidney, Hölderlin, Donne, the canon of love poets. They suffer the sadness of comparison. "Could *our* incredible marriage . . like all others' . . ?" trails off one of the sonnets, as if understanding that this is only one more love affair in a historical sequence of lovers and their sonnets, of passions bound by time. The poems are aware of the world around them. Both lovers were married to other people, and while Berryman considered submitting a few of them to magazines under the pseudonym Alan Fury, he withheld them from publication. Twenty years later, after he had found success—77 *Dream Songs* was published in 1964 and won the Pulitzer Prize for Poetry—he returned to these sonnets and edited them for publication. He replaced the repeated name "Chris" with the almost rhyming "Lise," presumably to disguise his lover's identity, but what is most odd about this—and what reveals most about Berryman's deep ambivalence toward the question of confession—is that having begun to erase the traces of her identity, he only went halfway. He changed her name but not the elaborate system of puns and echoes built upon that name. The eighteenth sonnet, for example, now addresses: "You, Lise, *contrite* I never thought to see, / Whom nothing fazes, no *crise* can disconcert." He retains sonnet 87, which is an acrostic: the first letter of each line spells out "I CHRIS AND I JOHN." This is a halfhearted discretion, as if he wanted to be caught. This is the poetic equivalent of the married man who leaves his lover's lipstick on his collar.

How does the poet stand in relation to his subject? What does he owe, and what is his duty? These are the questions behind confessional poetry, and they are the questions that Berryman is working out. In late March 1948 Berryman wrote the first two stanzas of a new, long poem. It opens with a question as the poet directly addresses his subject:

The Governor your husband lived so long
moved you not, restless, waiting for him?

Anne Bradstreet is sometimes described as the first American poet. She arrived in New England in 1630 and her first volume of verse was published in 1650. Berryman calls to her across the centuries:

> Out of maize & air
> your body's made, and moves. I summon, see,
> from the centuries it.
> I think you won't stay

he fears, but she comes to him. In the fifth stanza, her voice begins to take over. "By the week we landed we were, most, used up," she recounts, and tells him of her life, her early days in the New World, the first winters, and—in a rightly celebrated passage—the birth of her first child:

> One proud tug greens Heaven. Marvellous,
> unforbidding Majesty.
> Swell, imperious bells. I fly.

Soon, she will not remain confined to history. The poet speaks to her, and she replies, flirting with him: "You must not love me, but"—she pauses—"I do not bid you cease."

"Homage to Mistress Bradstreet" remains a startlingly bold poem, even today. It jumbles time, wrong-footing the reader with its inverted syntax and strange ellipses. Anne Bradstreet sees the ship on which they came to the New World rotting:

> The Lady Arbella dying—
> dyings—at which my heart   rose, but I did submit.

History is overwhelming the present here. She asks him, "Sing a concord of our thought," and Berryman replies: "I am drowning in this past." He goes on to describe a strange vision, a nightmare of guilt:

> I trundle the bodies, on the iron bars,
> over that fire backward & forth; they burn;

bits fall. I wonder if
I killed them.

She replies: "Dreams! You are good."

The first of the Dream Songs begins:

Huffy Henry hid   the day,
unappeasable Henry sulked.
I see his point,—a trying to put things over.

The pieces come from elsewhere, but their density is new. A slang expression and a strange name; two characters, at least one of which is mysterious; meter jumping between iambs and trochees and a fluid, unusual syntax. The gap in the first line appears to convert an intransitive into a transitive verb, although of course it doesn't; rather, it only thwarts our expectation of reliable, decipherable grammar. What is Henry hiding? Or where? Perhaps he's hiding (something) inside that space in the line. We move from past to present tense, and by the second half of the third line the pronouns have dissolved.

In October 1954, Berryman moved to Minneapolis, to an apartment near a lake, and in the winter when it froze he liked to walk out on the ice. He began to keep a journal of his dreams. By the summer, he had 650 pages of dream analysis. In June 1955, he signed a contract for two books with Farrar, Straus & Cudahy. The first was *Homage to Mistress Bradstreet*, which was published in October 1956; the second was a biography of Shakespeare. Berryman never finished this book. Instead, he began writing what he called from the start "dream songs," which he did almost exclusively for the next fifteen years, at the rate of sometimes two a day. It is worth taking a short detour into the book that Berryman did not write to understand the ones he did.

Berryman began working on Shakespeare in early 1937, in Cambridge. Specifically, he was interested in the textual states and chronology of the plays, which is a dry subfield of literary criticism but which he found enthralling. In February 1937 he wrote: "It's awfully silly ever to do anything but read Shakespeare," and this might sound like only a young snob's boast, but he seems to have meant it. In May 1944 he won a fellowship from the Rockefeller Foundation, for Shakespeare textual study; he worked by night in a small basement office in the Princeton University library, and when it was locked he climbed in and out through a window. In 1952 he was awarded a grant from the Guggenheim Foundation "for the critical study of Shakespeare," and in 1958 he claimed to have settled the date of Shakespeare's early play *The Two Gentlemen of Verona*: "It is late 1592—early 1593 and I can prove it." In 1964 he won another grant, to complete the book that was now called "Shakespeare's Friend," and he went to Washington to do research but spent all his time in bars. In 1969, on leaving a rehabilitation clinic: "A few months ought to see my biography at 500–600 pages." In February 1970 he wrote a short lyric: "I'm hot these 20 yrs. on his collaborator / in *The Taming of the Shrew*." In May 1970, on entering a treatment program for alcoholism, he made a list of "replacements for drinking," and the first item was: "work on my Shakespeare biography mornings & afternoons." In June 1971, he applied for and won a grant from the National Endowment for the Humanities, for work on the book that was now called "Shakespeare's Reality." On 17 December of that year, he wrote a note: "I thought new disappointments impossible but last night suddenly doubted if I really *have* a book 'Shakespeare's Reality' at all, despite all these years."

His life—it is not glamorous to say so—was a parade of grants and fellowships. When he was in trouble, the academic world came to rescue him. On his return from Cambridge, he taught in the English department at Wayne University in Michigan, and was hired by Harvard in 1940. He moved on to Princeton in 1943, where he taught creative writing. He lectured at the University of Cincinnati in 1952 and taught briefly at the Iowa Writers' Workshop in Iowa in 1954, and in 1955 he became a lecturer in humanities at the University of Minnesota. These universities provided the financial support that enabled him to become a poet, and something more than this. His biographer John Haffenden quotes one of Berryman's students at Princeton, who remembered

Berryman wearing a long striped scarf and reading a book while he walked across campus. "He seemed above all things donnish," said the student: "I remember someone saying nobody ever looked so much a poet."

He was "donnish," like a don, and he looked like a poet: the universities gave Berryman a role to play and to play against. *The Dream Songs* is the product of this close, bookish world: the poems are specific on the protocols and hierarchies of academic life. "Hey, out there!" begins one:

> assistant professors, full,
> associates,—instructors—others—any—
> I have a sing to shay.
> We are assembled here in the capital
> city for Dull—and one professor's wife is Mary—
> at Christmastide, hey!

This dream song has the title "MLA," which is the annual conference of English departments in U.S. universities. The members of the Modern Language Association meet just after Christmas each year, and they jostle for status and jobs; assistant professors seek to rise in rank to associate professors. Later, in Dream Song 373, he returns to the joke as he imagines the scholars who will study him after his death:

> will they set up a tumult in his praise
> will assistant professors become associates
> by working on his works?

He mocks the things he knows and loves.

John Haffenden's painstaking 1999 collection of Berryman's various academic writings on Shakespeare reveals much about the poet. His early work on textual states was built upon his assumption that the differing texts of Shakespeare's plays are different because they have been reconstructed by the actors who first appeared in them, and once we think of these as people's voices rather than texts, then we might be able to retrieve the original. As he wrote in February 1946: "One must emend through the error to the copy, and through that to the actor, hoping to reach Shakespeare." For Berryman, textual scholarship was an art of hearing human voices. Later, he became obsessed with tracking down Shakespeare's collaborators and coauthors, and after this he sought to write a biography: describing himself as "sick of quarter-Shakespeares," he wanted to tell the whole story of the man. He is always seeking people, and when he came to interpret the plays he found them to be testaments of intimate experience. "Shakespeare was a man whose son died, who was publicly ridiculed and insulted, who followed a degrading occupation," he wrote: "He wrote many personal poems about some of these things." In a superb lecture called "The Crisis," Berryman speculated that Shakespeare in early middle age suffered a nervous collapse, and he traces the symptoms through several plays, particularly *Hamlet*. Berryman read Shakespeare as the original confessional poet.

Shakespeare gave Berryman an image of what a poet might be; he taught him also how to sound. In a moving elegy published in *The New York Review of Books*, Robert Lowell recalled a summer day spent with Berryman: "John could quote with vibrance to all lengths, even prose, even late Shakespeare, to show me what could be done with disrupted and mended syntax. This was the start of his real style." Shakespeare's late plays are marked by a thickening of language as images pile upon one another and nouns are switched with verbs, and the sense is hard to follow. As a single example, here is the description of a swimmer from *The Tempest*:

> his bold head
> 'Bove the contentious waves he kept, and oared
> Himself with his good arms in lusty stroke
> To th' shore, that o'er his wave-worn basis bowed,
> As stooping to relieve him.

The convoluted phrasing of the *Dream Songs* follows this as Berryman defers the subject from each description; his songs are often tiny plays, with two speakers, dialogue, and heightened dramatic tension.

He borrows words and phrases, too, particularly from the trage-
dies. Dream Song 91 begins, "Noises from underground made gibber
some," and this follows *Hamlet* as Horatio describes a night in ancient
Rome when "[t]he graves stood tenantless, and the sheeted dead / Did
squeak and gibber in the Roman streets." In Dream Song 48 Henry is
"Cawdor-uneasy, disambitious," and he is recalling *Macbeth*; in 49, Berry-
man's question, "How come he sleeps & sleeps and sleeps, waking like
death: / locate the restorations of which we hear / as of profound sleep,"
follows the play's famous account of sleep as "[t]he death of each day's
life . . . Balm of hurt minds, great nature's second course." The imagery
of *King Lear* runs throughout the *Dream Songs*, from the "Thumbs into
eyes" that Henry fears in 226 to the haunting question "Who's king
these nights?" in 85. When Henry suffers from a "brain on fire" he is
also Lear, "bound / Upon a wheel of fire," and even more directly Berry-
man notes, "'O get up & go in' / somewhere once I heard," which is an
almost-quotation from the play. The examples continue; Berryman's
poetry awaits the fully annotated scholarly edition he would have loved.
I suggested earlier that Berryman never completed his book on Shake-
speare, but this is of course untrue. John Berryman finished a great
work of Shakespeare scholarship and criticism. It is called *The Dream
Songs*.

The gorgeous convolution of late Shakespeare is certainly one source
of the Dream Song style; a second is closer to home. Writing in *The
Harvard Advocate* in the spring of 1969, Adrienne Rich declared, "A
new language is evolving in the heads of some Americans who use
English." Where other countries have "the security of a native tongue,
of a Dictionary," Americans must improvise their own language out of
the basic elements of another. The American language is

> this mad amalgam of ballad-idiom (ours via Appalachia),
> Shakespeherian rag, Gerard Manley Hopkins in a delirium of
> syntactical reversals, nigger-talk, blues talk, hip-talk engen-
> dered from both, Miltonic diction, Calypso, bureaucratiana,
> pure blurted Anglo-Saxon.

Only two men, Rich concludes, understand exactly what this language is: Bob Dylan and John Berryman. Both changed their names; both found long-worked-for success in 1965, which was the year that Dylan famously went electric and that Berryman won a Pulitzer for 77 *Dream Songs*. Both created by theft, by allusion and borrowing, and both wrote songs.

In Cambridge in 1936, Berryman was carefully listening to voices. He was surrounded by English voices, which he sometimes found hard to follow. "The rhythms of speech are very different," he wrote to his mother not long after he had arrived: "Unless I attend very closely, I sometimes fail to understand several sentences at a time." He was also paying new attention to the few American accents he heard. They were unusual, like rare flowers, and distance may make the familiar strange. He was reading, he went on, H. L. Mencken's book *The American Language*: the fourth edition had just been published, and he described it as "really an extraordinary job, and a very good thing to be reading when I hear the island varieties of English so continually." What he hears his Cambridge classmates speaking is not proper English, that is, but one dialect of it: one of the "island varieties." This is in miniature the argument of Mencken's combative and sprawling book. The American language is, for Mencken, marked by three characteristics. It is uniform, across the country; it is impatient with the rules of grammar; and it likes to borrow and to invent words. The first colonists needed new words for the things they had never seen before, so they borrowed "moose," "skunk," and "raccoon" from the Native Americans, and for the same reason they took words from Spanish. Mencken gives the example of "cockroach."

Mencken quotes a 1914 study of the grammar used by students at twelve schools in Kansas City. "Its examination threw a brilliant light upon the speech actually employed by children near the end of their schooling in a typical American city," he notes; this is the American language captured in the year of Berryman's birth, and the study's list of common errors reads now like a taxonomy of Dream Song style. The writings of these high school students displayed syntactical redundancy; there was incorrect use of mood, and a confusion of tenses; they misused comparatives and superlatives, and exchanged adjectives for adverbs. The verb often failed to agree with its subject, both in number and in person, and the pronoun often failed to correspond to its noun. "The chief grammatical peculiarities of spoken American lie . . . among the verbs and pronouns," Mencken summarizes, and it is precisely these uses of verbs and pronouns "which set off the Common speech very sharply from both correct English and correct American." Pronouns tell us who is speaking and what is spoken of; verbs clarify the actions taking place; in that first Dream Song we are told, "What he has now to say is a long / wonder the world can bear & be." The sense is clear but the grammar is not. Berryman, who spoke with an English accent, wrote the Dream Songs in American.

This study of schoolchildren thinks in terms of errors, but Mencken does not share this prejudice, nor does Berryman: for both, a break in proper grammar is an opportunity, not a fault. In 1950, Berryman published a study of Stephen Crane; the book reads as closer to autobiography than biography, for Berryman seems to be writing as much about himself as his subject. Here he defines a writer as "a man alone in a room with the English language, trying to get human feelings right," and here he considers Crane's wayward grammar, particularly in his famous novel *The Red Badge of Courage*. "Crane's grammatical sins consist mostly of difficulty in agreement, in reference, and in word order," he writes, and observes that this at times leads Crane to "a gruesome awkwardness." However: "This writer does not aim, as a rule, at smoothness, and of his oddest sentences some seem calculated." He adds, as a rationale for this careful and creative abuse of the rules of grammar, one final proof: Of all writers, Shakespeare's grammar "was flexible."

The Dream Songs blur tenses, places, and people; they are not smooth. "A shallow lake, with many waterbirds," begins Dream Song 101, and beneath the line is the footstep of iambic pentameter, Shakespeare's meter; the rest of the poem does not conform to this, but it is established here at the start and then recalled, like a ghost, throughout. We are at a lake: it is unusual for a Dream Song to begin with such a simple setting and soon it takes back even this. "I was showing Mother around, / An extraordinary vivid dream," it goes on, and the line break switches the meaning. The speaker was showing his mother around the lake in his dream; the speaker was showing his dream to his mother.

In the fourth line three more characters appear: "Betty & Douglas, and Don." "He showed me around," adds the speaker in an attempt at clarification, but now we are in a tangle of dreams and characters. A policeman arrives: "I askt if he ever saw / the inmates." There was some trouble—"Don was late home"—but the poem refuses to explain. "I can't go into the meaning of the dream," the speaker says, "except to say a sense of total LOSS / afflicted me thereof," and we are back in a loose iambic pentameter. The poem's informality of subject and association dances against a hard poetic formality. This is something like what Shakespearean American might be: a possible language for poetry, traditional and innovative, rich and strange.

In the end, John Berryman did two things, and in so doing he summarized two great themes of his life's work. These are a gift to his biographers and biographically minded interpreters, for they put a neat and legible stop upon the fluid, misunderstanding-filled story of his life. They make it all look inevitable in retrospect. In Berryman's last collections of poems—*Love & Fame* (1970), and the posthumously published *Delusions, Etc.* (1972)—along with his uncollected late poems, we can feel the poet sorting and arranging the materials of his unsettled life.

First he looked back. *Love & Fame* and *Delusions, Etc.* set out a verse autobiography as Berryman ranges over his time and his memories of what had made him.

> I fell in love with a girl.
> O and a gash.
> I'll bet she now has seven lousy children.
> (I've three myself, one being off the record.)

So begins *Love & Fame*, and the poems here are in loose quatrains, sometimes casually rhymed, informal and powerful. They consider Berryman's young romantic and sexual entanglements, and his longing to be a poet. Often the desire for girls and the desire for literary fame are joined. "Images of Elspeth" begins:

> O when I grunted, over lines and her,
> my Muse a nymphet & my girl with men
> older, of money, continually
> lawyers & so, myself a flat-broke Junior.

This collection displays what Berryman calls in that same poem "a sense of humour / fatal to bardic pretension." He acknowledges his youthful absurdity. In another he recalls of his earliest poetry: "I wrote mostly about death." Blessed by wryness, the older man looks back, with affection, upon who he once was.

Berryman had of course done this before. In 1966, deciding to publish the cycle of sonnets he had written twenty years earlier, he looked back upon his previous self. In a poem added to the cycle at the time of publication, he describes writing these sonnets: "He made, a thousand years ago, a-many songs / for an Excellent lady, wif whom he was in wuv." The childish spelling and past tense distance the younger man; twenty years become a thousand. In the autobiographical poems from *Love & Fame* and *Delusions, Etc.* he is warmer toward the younger man. What is perhaps most striking about these late poems is that he is writing the voice of his earlier self even while that younger self is— as an apprentice Great Poet—trying to work out what his voice is going to sound like. It is a switchback trick of sympathetic recall and a careful balancing act. He was hopeful and a little ridiculous, back when he was setting out. In "Two Organs," he recalls:

> I didn't want my next poem to be *exactly* like Yeats
> or exactly like Auden
> since in that case where the hell was *I*?

But of course he learned by imitation; those italics lightly spoof his wish for originality.

It might be tempting to read these late poems as the moment Berryman at last became a confessional poet. He narrates his studies in Cambridge and his return to the United States. He finds success, has affairs and a first breakdown. He is increasingly explicit, about both sex and his life; he includes his home address in Minneapolis in one poem. But he warns: "I am not writing an autobiography-in-verse, my friends," and we may see these poems in two slightly different contexts. Berryman was first admitted to the hospital for alcoholism in 1959, and for the rest of his life he was regularly in treatment: most often at the Abbott Hospital in Minneapolis, where he wrote many Dream Songs ("I prop on the costly bed & dream of my wife"), and the Intensive Alcohol Treatment Center at St. Mary's Hospital in the same city. In 1970 he joined Alcoholics Anonymous. Their Twelve Steps of recovery insist upon self-evaluation. At Step Four, patients "[m]ade a searching and fearless inventory of ourselves," and at Step Five "[a]dmitted to God, to ourselves, and to another human being the exact nature of our wrongs." These are also exercises for a writer: during 1971, as he was writing these last poems, Berryman was simultaneously at work on a novel— about a man undergoing treatment for alcoholism—called *Recovery*. The novel, while unfinished, is structured upon the steps of treatment.

He was not thinking only of the shape of his own life, however. In his late poems Berryman turned to writing the lives of others, poets and artists, historical figures he admired. *Delusions, Etc.* includes a memorial poem for Dylan Thomas and the birthday song for Emily Dickinson; he wrote a biographical sketch of George Washington in seven fragments and a cycle of mostly quatrains in which he addresses Beethoven. He describes Beethoven's famous late style: "Straightforward staves, dark bars, / late motions toward the illegible." In these last works—his own late style—Berryman is again experimenting with how to plot a life in poetry. Among the unpublished works collected by John Haffenden in the posthumous *Henry's Fate* is a poem in which Berryman describes Che Guevara as an almost holy, Christlike figure. "I'm screwed if I'll praise you," he declares to him: "you open a hope / we're not contemptible necessity."

Second, he embraced the end. His last two collections each include a cycle of devotional verse: "Eleven Addresses to the Lord" and the moving "Opus Dei," which is composed of nine poems following the order of Latin liturgical hours. Like all devotional verse—and Berryman here sounds at times like George Herbert, perhaps the greatest devotional poet of all—these poems contemplate the limits of the self, and human life. Again, this embrace of a higher power is one central strand in the practice established by Alcoholics Anonymous: Step Two instructs, "Believe that a Power greater than ourselves could restore us to sanity," and the final step only comes once the patient has undergone "a spiritual awakening." Like recovery, devotion is the art of imagining what might come next, outside this known world.

This is a new poetic. Here, he is turning away from the self. In "Matins":

> However, lo, across what wilderness
> in vincible ignorance past forty years
> lost to (as now I see) Your sorrowing
> I strayed abhorrent, blazing with my Self.

Here, he is trying to submit. In "Nones":

> I am olding & ignorant, and the work is great,
> daylight is long, will ever I be done,
> for the work is not for man, but the Lord God.
> Now I have prepared with all my might for it

The drama and the tension—the beauty—of these late poems is that of a man torn between the fascinations of the self and the chance of a greater order. He is never wholly convinced. He is at best a "pseudo-monk," as he calls himself in "Terce," but the cycle of prayers enacts a drama of submission. This is not easy. It ends: "This fireless house / lies down at Your disposal as usual! Amen!"

On the morning of Friday, January 7, 1972, Berryman took the bus from his home to the university, but instead of going to his office he walked onto the Washington Avenue Bridge. He climbed over the railing, and then—according to one witness—waved goodbye before jumping. His body landed on the embankment of the west side of the Mississippi River. This great poet of shifting personalities could only be identified by the blank check in his pocket and his glasses, which had his name on the frame.

There is a strong temptation to read Berryman's life as tragic, to see in it a parable of art and suffering. His biographers and critics find it hard to resist this precisely because Berryman himself leads them to it. In 1955, he wrote a fragmentary memoir of his school days, and he called it "It Hurts to Learn Anything": throughout his life he repeatedly expressed his belief in a kind of equation of suffering and creativity. In 1965, when asked by a newspaper interviewer about the elements of good poetry, he replied: "Imagination, love, intellect—and pain. Yes, you've got to know pain." He repeated this in his interview with *The Paris Review*, which was carried out in the fall of 1970. There, he said: "The artist is extremely lucky who is presented with the worst possible ordeal which will not actually kill him." This is a Romantic idea, of authority won by hurt, and poetry as dark knowledge, and it is bound up with Berryman's own brooding upon his death. In a poem from the late 1950s called "The Poet's Final Instructions," he explains his wishes for his funeral: "Bury me in a hole, and give a cheer, / near Cedar on Lake Street, where the used cars live." In his suicide, Berryman seemed to write a fit conclusion to this version of his life.

I don't want to leave him like this, however, as a poet of retrospect and endings, as an artist of the grave. This misses something his writing life powerfully was: a joy of voices, antic and alive. There is the tragic urge, but there is also its counter: the pull toward life. In a very late Dream Song—written, according to his biographer Paul Mariani, in 1969, after the publication of *His Toy, His Dream, His Rest*, which completes the Dream Songs—Berryman considered this divided sense:

A human personality, that's impossible.
The lines of nature & of will, that's impossible.
I give the whole thing up.

His larger project, across his life, was the attempt to capture in verse "a human personality," and the challenge remained daunting. But then he turns before the poem finishes:

Only there resides a living voice
which if we can make we make it out of choice
not giving the whole thing up.

—Daniel Swift

FROM

The Dispossessed

(1948)

Winter Landscape

The three men coming down the winter hill
In brown, with tall poles and a pack of hounds
At heel, through the arrangement of the trees,
Past the five figures at the burning straw,
Returning cold and silent to their town,

Returning to the drifted snow, the rink
Lively with children, to the older men,
The long companions they can never reach,
The blue light, men with ladders, by the church
The sledge and shadow in the twilit street,

Are not aware that in the sandy time
To come, the evil waste of history
Outstretched, they will be seen upon the brow
Of that same hill: when all their company
Will have been irrecoverably lost,

These men, this particular three in brown
Witnessed by birds will keep the scene and say
By their configuration with the trees,
The small bridge, the red houses and the fire,
What place, what time, what morning occasion

Sent them into the wood, a pack of hounds
At heel and the tall poles upon their shoulders,
Thence to return as now we see them and
Ankle-deep in snow down the winter hill
Descend, while three birds watch and the fourth flies.

A Point of Age, Part I

At twenty-five a man is on his way.
The desolate childhood smokes on the dead hill,
My adolescent brothels are shut down
For industry has moved out of that town;
Only the time-dishonoured beggars and
The flat policemen, victims, I see still.
Twenty-five is a time to move away.

The travelling hands upon the tower call,
The clock-face telescopes a long desire:
Out of the city as the autos stream
I watch, I whisper, Is it time . . time?
Fog is enveloping the bridges, lodgers
Shoulder and fist each other in the mire
Where later, leaves, untidy lives will fall.

Companions, travellers, by luck, by fault
Whose none can ever decide, friends I had
Have frozen back or slipt ahead or let
Landscape juggle their destinations, slut
Solace and drink drown the degraded eye.
The fog is settling and the night falls, sad,
Across the forward shadows where friends halt.

Images are the mind's life, and they change.
How to arrange it—what can one afford
When ghosts and goods tether the twitching will
Where it has stood content and would stand still
If time's map bore the brat of time intact?
Odysseys I examine, bed on a board,
Heartbreak familiar as the heart is strange.

In the city of the stranger I discovered
Strike and corruption: cars reared on the bench
To horn their justice at the citizen's head
And hallow the citizen deaf, half-dead.
The quiet man from his own window saw
Insane wind take the ash, his favourite branch
Wrench, crack; the hawk came down, the raven hovered.

Slow spent stars wheel and dwindle where I fell.
Physicians are a constellation where
The blown brain sits a fascist to the heart.
Late, it is late, and it is time to start.
Sanction the civic woe, deal with your dear,
Convince the stranger: none of us is well.
We must travel in the direction of our fear.

The Ball Poem

What is the boy now, who has lost his ball,
What, what is he to do? I saw it go
Merrily bouncing, down the street, and then
Merrily over—there it is in the water!
No use to say 'O there are other balls':
An ultimate shaking grief fixes the boy
As he stands rigid, trembling, staring down
All his young days into the harbour where
His ball went. I would not intrude on him,
A dime, another ball, is worthless. Now
He senses first responsibility
In a world of possessions. People will take balls,
Balls will be lost always, little boy,
And no one buys a ball back. Money is external.
He is learning, well behind his desperate eyes,
The epistemology of loss, how to stand up
Knowing what every man must one day know
And most know many days, how to stand up
And gradually light returns to the street,
A whistle blows, the ball is out of sight,
Soon part of me will explore the deep and dark
Floor of the harbour . . I am everywhere,
I suffer and move, my mind and my heart move
With all that move me, under the water
Or whistling, I am not a little boy.

The Possessed

This afternoon, discomfortable dead
Drift into doorways, lounge, across the bridge,
Whittling memory at the water's edge,
And watch. This is what you inherited.

Random they are, but hairy, for they chafe
All in their eye, enlarging like a slide;
Spectral as men once met or crucified,
And kind. Until the sun sets you are safe.

A prey to your most awkward reflection,
Loose-limbed before the fire you sit appalled.
And think that by your error you have called
These to you. Look! the light will soon be gone.

Excited see from the window the men fade
In the twilight; reappear two doors down.
Suppose them well acquainted with the town
Who built it. Do you fumble in the shade?

The key was lost, remember, yesterday,
Or stolen,—undergraduates perhaps;
But all men are their colleagues, and eclipse
Very like dusk. It is too late to pray.

There was a time crepuscular was mild,
The hour for tea, acquaintances, and fall
Away of all day's difficulties, all
Discouragement. Weep, you are not a child.

The equine hour rears, no further friend,
Intolerant, foam-lathered, pregnant with
Mysterious grave watchers in their wrath
Let into tired Troy. You are near the end.

Midsummer Common loses its last gold,
And grey is there. The sun slants down behind
A certain cinema, and the world is blind
But more dangerous. It is growing cold.

Light all the lights, heap wood upon the fire
To banish shadow. Draw the curtains tight.
But sightless eyes will lean through and wide night
Darken this room of yours. As you desire.

Think on your sins with all intensity.
The men are on the stair, they will not wait.
There is a paper-knife to penetrate
Heart & guilt together. Do it quickly.

Parting as Descent

The sun rushed up the sky; the taxi flew;
There was a kind of fever on the clock
That morning. We arrived at Waterloo
With time to spare and couldn't find my track.

The bitter coffee in a small café
Gave us our conversation. When the train
Began to move, I saw you turn away
And vanish, and the vessels in my brain

Burst, the train roared, the other travellers
In flames leapt, burning on the tilted air
Che si cruccia, I heard the devils curse
And shriek with joy in that place beyond prayer.

The Animal Trainer (2)

I told him: The time has come, I must be gone.
It is time to leave the circus and circus days,
The admissions, the menagerie, the drums,
Excitements of disappointment and praise.
In a suburb of the spirit I shall seize
The steady and exalted light of the sun
And live there, out of the tension that decays,
Until I become a man alone of noon.

Heart said: Can you do without these animals?
The looking, licking, smelling animals?
The friendly fumbling beast? The listening one?
The standing up and worst of animals?
What will become of you in the pure light
When all your enemies are gone, and gone
The inexhaustible prospect of the night?

—But the night is now the body of my fear,
These animals are my distraction! Once
Let me escape the smells and cages here,
Once let me stand naked in the sun,
All their performances will be forgotten.
I shall concentrate in the sunlight there.

Said the conservative Heart: These animals
Are occupation, food for you, your love
And your despair, responsibility:
They are the travellers by which you live.
Without you they will pace and pine, or die.

—What soul-delighting tasks do they perform?
They quarrel, snort, leap, lie down, their delight
Merely a punctual meal and to be warm.
Justify their existence in the night!

—The animals are coupling, and they cry
'The circus *is*, it is our mystery,
It is a world of dark where animals die.'

—Animals little and large, be still, be still:
I'll stay with you. Suburb and sun are pale.

—Animals are your destruction, and your will.

Desire Is a World by Night

The history of strangers in their dreams
Being irresponsible, is fun for men,
Whose sons are neither at the Front nor frame
Humiliating weakness to keep at home
Nor wince on principle, wearing mother grey,
Honoured by radicals. When the mind is free
The catechetical mind can mince and tear
Contemptible vermin from a stranger's hair
And then sleep.

                In our parents' dreams we see
Vigour abutting on senility,
Stiff blood, and weathered with the years, poor vane;
Unfortunate but inescapable.
Although this wind bullies the windowpane
Are the children to be kept responsible
For the world's decay? Carefully we choose
Our fathers, carefully we cut out those
On whom to exert the politics of praise.

Heard after dinner, in defenceless ease,
The dreams of friends can puzzle, dazzle us
With endless journeys through unfriendly snow,
Malevolent faces that appear and frown
Where nothing was expected, the sudden stain
On spotless window-ledges; these we take
Chuckling, but take them with us when we go,
To study in secret, late, brooding, looking
For trails and parallels. We have a stake
In this particular region, and we look

Excitedly for situations that we know.
—The disinterested man has gone abroad;
Winter is on the by-way where he rode
Erect and alone, summery years ago.

When we dream, paraphrase, analysis
Exhaust the crannies of the night. We stare,
Fresh sweat upon our foreheads, as they fade:
The melancholy and terror of avenues
Where long no single man has moved, but play
Under the arc-lights gangs of the grey dead
Running directionless. That bright blank place
Advances with us into fearful day,
Heady and insuppressible. Call in friends,
They grin and carry it carefully away,—
The fathers can't be trusted,—strangers wear
Their strengths, and visor. Last, authority,
The Listener borrow from an English grave
To solve our hatred and our bitterness . .
The foul and absurd to solace or dismay.
All this will never appear; we will not say;
Let the evidence be buried in a cave
Off the main road. If anyone could see
The white scalp of that passionate will and those
Sullen desires, he would stumble, dumb,
Retreat into the time from which he came
Counting upon his fingers and his toes.

The Moon and the Night and the Men

On the night of the Belgian surrender the moon rose
Late, a delayed moon, and a violent moon
For the English or the American beholder;
The French beholder. It was a cold night,
People put on their wraps, the troops were cold
No doubt, despite the calendar, no doubt
Numbers of refugees coughed, and the sight
Or sound of some killed others. A cold night.

On Outer Drive there was an accident:
A stupid well-intentioned man turned sharp
Right and abruptly he became an angel
Fingering an unfamiliar harp,
Or screamed in hell, or was nothing at all.
Do not imagine this is unimportant.
He was a part of the night, part of the land,
Part of the bitter and exhausted ground
Out of which memory grows.

              Michael and I
Stared at each other over chess, and spoke
As little as possible, and drank and played.
The chessmen caught in the European eye,
Neither of us I think had a free look
Although the game was fair. The move one made
It was difficult at last to keep one's mind on.
'Hurt and unhappy' said the man in London.
We said to each other, The time is coming near
When none shall have books or music, none his dear,

And only a fool will speak aloud his mind.
History is approaching a speechless end,
As Henry Adams said. Adams was right.

All this occurred on the night when Leopold
Fulfilled the treachery four years before
Begun—or was he well-intentioned, more
Roadmaker to hell than king? At any rate,
The moon came up late and the night was cold,
Many men died—although we know the fate
Of none, nor of anyone, and the war
Goes on, and the moon in the breast of man is cold.

from *The Nervous Songs*

YOUNG WOMAN'S SONG

The round and smooth, my body in my bath,
If someone else would like it too.—I did,
I wanted T. to think 'How interesting'
Although I hate his voice and face, hate both.
I hate this something like a bobbing cork
Not going. I want something to hang to.—

A fierce wind roaring high up in the bare
Branches of trees,—I suppose it was lust
But it was holy and awful. All day I thought
I am a bobbing cork, irresponsible child
Loose on the waters.—What have you done at last?
A little work, a little vague chat.

I want that £3.10 hat terribly.—
What I am looking for (*I am*) may be
Happening in the gaps of what I know.
The full moon does go with you as yóu go.
Where am I going? I am not afraid . .
Only I would be lifted lost in the flood.

THE SONG OF THE DEMENTED PRIEST

I put those things there.—See them burn.
The emerald the azure and the gold
Hiss and crack, the blues & greens of the world
As if I were tired. Someone interferes
Everywhere with me. The clouds, the clouds are torn
In ways I do not understand or love.

Licking my long lips, I looked upon God
And he flamed and he was friendlier
Than you were, and he was small. Showing me
Serpents and thin flowers; these were cold.
Dominion waved & glittered like the flare
From ice under a small sun. I wonder.

Afterward the violent and formal dancers
Came out, shaking their pithless heads.
I would instruct them but I cannot now,—
Because of the elements. They rise and move,
I nod a dance and they dance in the rain
In my red coat. I am the king of the dead.

A PROFESSOR'S SONG

(. . rabid or dog-dull.) Let me tell you how
The Eighteenth Century couplet ended. Now
Tell me. Troll me the sources of that Song—
Assigned last week—by Blake. Come, come along,
Gentlemen. (Fidget and huddle, do. Squint soon.)
I want to end these fellows all by noon.

'That deep romantic chasm'—an early use;
The word is from the French, by our abuse
Fished out a bit. (Red all your eyes. O when?)
'A poet is a man speaking to men':
But I am then a poet, am I not?—
Ha ha. The radiator, please. Well, what?

Alive now—no—Blake would have written prose,
But movement following movement crisply flows,
So much the better, better the much so,
As burbleth Mozart. Twelve. The class can go.
Until I meet you, then, in Upper Hell
Convulsed, foaming immortal blood: farewell.

THE SONG OF THE TORTURED GIRL

After a little I could not have told—
But no one asked me this—why I was there.
I asked. The ceiling of that place was high
And there were sudden noises, which I made.
I must have stayed there a long time today:
My cup of soup was gone when they brought me back.

Often 'Nothing worse now can come to us'
I thought, the winter the young men stayed away,
My uncle died, and mother broke her crutch.
And then the strange room where the brightest light
Does not shine on the strange men: shines on me.
I feel them stretch my youth and throw a switch.

Through leafless branches the sweet wind blows
Making a mild sound, softer than a moan;
High in a pass once where we put our tent,
Minutes I lay awake to hear my joy.
—I no longer remember what they want.—
Minutes I lay awake to hear my joy.

The Lightning

Sick with the lightning lay my sister-in-law,
Concealing it from her children, when I came.
What I could, did, helpless with what I saw.

Analysands all, and the rest ought to be,
The friends my innocence cherished, and you and I,
Darling,—the friends I qualm and cherish and see.

. . The fattest nation!—wé do not thrive fat
But facile in the scale with all we rise
And shift a breakfast, and there is shame in that.

And labour sweats with vice at the top, and two
Bullies are bristling. What he thought who thinks?
It is difficult to say what one will do.

Obstinate, gleams from the black world the gay and fair,
My love loves chocolate, she loves also me,
And the lightning dances, but I cannot despair.

New Year's Eve

The grey girl who had not been singing stopped,
And a brave new no-sound blew through acrid air.
I set my drink down, hard. Somebody slapped
Somebody's second wife somewhere,
Wheeling away to long to be alone.
I see the dragon of years is almost done,
Its claws loosen, its eyes
Crust now with tears & lust and a scale of lies.

A whisky-listless and excessive saint
Was expounding his position, whom I hung
Boy-glad in glowing heaven: he grows faint:
Hearing what song the sirens sung,
Sidelong he web-slid and some rich prose spun.
The tissue golden of the gifts undone
Surpassed the gifts. Miss Weirs
Whispers to me her international fears.

Intelligentsia milling. In a semi-German
(Our loss of Latin fractured how far our fate,—
Disinterested once, linkage once like a sermon)
I struggle to articulate
Why it is our promise breaks in pieces early.
The Muses' visitants come soon, go surly
With liquor & mirrors away
In this land wealthy & casual as a holiday.

Whom the Bitch winks at. Most of us are linsey-
woolsey workmen, grandiose, and slack.
On m'analyse, the key to secrets. Kinsey

Shortly will tell us sharply back
Habits we stuttered. How revive to join
(Great evils grieve beneath : eye Caesar's coin)
And lure a while more home
The vivid wanderers, uneasy with our shame?

Priests of the infinite! ah, not for long.
The dove whispers, and diminishes
Up the blue leagues. And no doubt we heard wrong—
Wax of our lives collects & dulls; but was
What we heard hurried as we memorized,
Or brightened, or adjusted? Undisguised
We pray our tongues & fingers
Record the strange word that blows suddenly and lingers.

Imagine a patience in the works of love
Luck sometimes visits. Ages we have sighed,
And cleave more sternly to a music of
Even this sore word 'genocide'.
Each to his own! Clockless & thankless dream
And labour Makers, being what we seem.
Soon soon enough we turn
Our tools in; brownshirt Time chiefly our works will burn.

I remember: white fine flour everywhere whirled
Ceaselessly, wheels rolled, a slow thunder boomed,
And there were snowy men in the mill-world
With sparkling eyes, light hair uncombed,
And one of them was humming an old song,
Sack upon sack grew portly, until strong

Arms moved them on, by pairs,
And then the bell clanged and they ran like hares.

Scotch in his oxter, my Retarded One
Blows in before the midnight; freezing slush
Stamps off, off. Worst of years! . . no matter, begone;
Your slash and spells (in the sudden hush)
We see now we had to suffer some day, so
I cross the dragon with a blessing, low,
While the black blood slows. Clock-wise,
We clasp upon the stroke, kissing with happy cries.

Of 1947

Berryman's Sonnets

(1947, 1967)

{ *1* }

I wished, all the mild days of middle March
This special year, your blond good-nature might
(Lady) admit—kicking abruptly tight
With will and affection down your breast like starch—
Me to your story, in Spring, and stretch, and arch.
But who not flanks the wells of uncanny light
Sudden in bright sand towering? A bone sunned white.
Considering travellers bypass these and parch.

This came to less yes than an ice cream cone
Let sand . . though still my sense of it is brisk:
Blond silky cream, sweet cold, aches: a door shut.
Errors of order! Luck lies with the bone,
Who rushed (and rests) to meet your small mouth, risk
Your teeth irregular and passionate.

Your shining—where?—rays my wide room with gold;
Grey rooms all day, green streets I visited,
Blazed with you possible; other voices bred
Yours in my quick ear; when the rain was cold
Shiver it might make shoulders I behold
Sloping through kite-slipt hours, tingling. I said
A month since, 'I will see that cloud-gold head,
Those eyes lighten, and go by': then your thunder rolled.

Drowned all sound else, I come driven to learn
Fearful and happy, deafening rumours of
The complete conversations of the angels, now
As nude upon some warm lawn softly turn
Toward me the silences of your breasts . . My vow! . .
One knee unnerves the voyeur sky enough.

{ 7 }

I've found out why, that day, that suicide
From the Empire State falling on someone's car
Troubled you so; and why we quarrelled. War,
Illness, an accident, I can see (you cried)
But not this: what a bastard, not spring wide! . .
I said a man, life in his teeth, could care
Not much just whom he spat it on . . and far
Beyond my laugh we argued either side.

'One has a right not to be fallen on! . .'
(Our second meeting . . yellow you were wearing.)
Voices of our resistance and desire!
Did I divine then I must shortly run
Crazy with need to fall on you, despairing?
Did you bolt so, before it caught, our fire?

Great citadels whereon the gold sun falls
Miss you O Lise sequestered to the West
Which wears you Mayday lily at its breast,
Part and not part, proper to balls and brawls,
Plains, cities, or the yellow shore, not false
Anywhere, free, native and Danishest
Profane and elegant flower,—whom suggest
Frail and not frail, blond rocks and madrigals.

Once in the car (cave of our radical love)
Your darker hair I saw than golden hair
Above your thighs whiter than white-gold hair,
And where the dashboard lit faintly your least
Enlarged scene, O the midnight bloomed . . the East
Less gorgeous, wearing you like a long white glove!

I lift—lift you five States away your glass,
Wide of this bar you never graced, where none
Ever I know came, where what work is done
Even by these men I know not, where a brass
Police-car sign peers in, wet strange cars pass,
Soiled hangs the rag of day out over this town,
A juke-box brains air where I drink alone,
The spruce barkeep sports a toupee alas—

My glass I lift at six o'clock, my darling,
As you plotted . . Chinese couples shift in bed,
We shared today not even filthy weather,
Beasts in the hills their tigerish love are snarling,
Suddenly they clash, I blow my short ash red,
Grey eyes light! and we have our drink together.

They may suppose, because I would not cloy your ear—
If ever these songs by other ears are heard—
With 'love' and 'love', I loved you not, but blurred
Lust with strange images, warm, not quite sincere,
To switch a bedroom black. O mutineer
With me against these empty captains! gird
Your scorn again above all at *this* word
Pompous and vague on the stump of his career.

Also I fox 'heart', striking a modern breast
Hollow as a drum, and 'beauty' I taboo;
I want a verse fresh as a bubble breaks,
As little false . . . Blood of my sweet unrest
Runs all the same—I am in love with you—
Trapped in my rib-cage something throes and aches!

You should be gone in winter, that Nature mourn
With me your anarch separation, call-
ing warmth all with you: as more poetical
Than to be left biting the dog-days, lorn
Alone when all else burgeons, brides are born,
Children yet (some) begotten, every wall
Clasped by its vine here . . crony alcohol
Comfort as random as the unicorn.

Listen, for poets are feigned to lie, and I
For you a liar am a thousand times,
Scars of these months blazon like a decree:
I would have you—a liner pulls the sky—
Trust when I mumble me. Than gin-&-limes
You are cooler, darling, O come back to me.

Itself a lightning-flash ripping the 'dark
Backward' of you-before, you harrowed me
How you and the wild boy (larcener-to-be)
Took horses out one night, full in the stark
Pre-storm midnight blackness, for a lark,
At seventeen, drunk, and you whipt them madly
About the gulph's rim, lightning-split, with glee
About, about. A decade: . . I embark.

How can we know with whom we ride, or soon
Or later, ever? You . . what are yóu like?
A topic's occupied me months, month's mind.
But I more startled may, than who shrank down
And wiped his sharp eyes with a helpless look,
The great tears falling, when Odysseus struck him, find.

Darling I wait O in my upstairs box
O for your footfall, O for your footfáll
in the extreme heat—I don't mind at all,
it's silence has me and the no of clocks
keeping us isolated longer: rocks
did the first martyr and will do to stall
our enemies, I'll get up on the roof of the hall
and heave freely. The University of Soft Knocks

will headlines in the *Times* make: Fellow goes mad,
crowd panics, rhododendrons injured. Slow
will flow the obituaries while the facts get straight,
almost straight. He was in love and he was had.
That was it: he should have stuck to his own mate,
before he went a-coming across the sea-O.

{ *114* }

You come blonde visiting through the black air
knocking on my hinged lawn-level window
and you will come for years, above, below,
& through to interrupt my study where
I'm sweating it out like asterisks: so there,—
you are the text, my work's broken down so
I found, after my grandmother died, slow,
and I had flown far South to her funeral spare

but crowded with relations, I found her last
letter unopened, much less answered: shame
overcame me so far I paused & cried
in my underground study, for all the past
undone & never again to walk tall, lame
at the mercy of your presence to abide.

All we were going strong last night this time,
the *mots* were flying & the frozen daiquiris
were downing, supine on the floor lay Lise
listening to Schubert grievous & sublime,
my head was frantic with a following rime:
it was a good evening, an evening to please,
I kissed her in the kitchen—ecstasies—
among so much good we tamped down the crime,

The weather's changing. This morning was cold,
as I made for the grove, without expectation,
some hundred Sonnets in my pocket, old,
to read her if she came. Presently the sun
yellowed the pines & my lady came not
in blue jeans & a sweater. I sat down & wrote.

Homage to Mistress Bradstreet

(1953)

Homage to Mistress Bradstreet

{Born 1612 Anne Dudley, married at 16 Simon Bradstreet, a Cambridge man, steward to the Countess of Warwick and protégé of her father Thomas Dudley secretary to the Earl of Lincoln. Crossed in the Arbella, *1630, under Governor Winthrop.}*

1

The Governor your husband lived so long
moved you not, restless, waiting for him? Still,
you were a patient woman.—
I seem to see you pause here still:
Sylvester, Quarles, in moments odd you pored
before a fire at, bright eyes on the Lord,
all the children still.
'Simon . . .' Simon will listen while you read a Song.

2

Outside the New World winters in grand dark
white air lashing high thro' the virgin stands
foxes down foxholes sigh,
surely the English heart quails, stunned.
I doubt if Simon than this blast, that sea,
spares from his rigour for your poetry
more. We are on each other's hands
who care. Both of our worlds unhanded us. Lie stark,

3

thy eyes look to me mild. Out of maize & air
your body's made, and moves. I summon, see,
from the centuries it.
I think you won't stay. How do we
linger, diminished, in our lovers' air,
implausibly visible, to whom, a year,
years, over interims; or not;
to a long stranger; or not; shimmer & disappear.

4

Jaw-ript, rot with its wisdom, rending then;
then not. When the mouth dies, who misses you?
Your master never died,
Simon ah thirty years past you—
Pockmarkt & westward staring on a haggard deck
it seems I find you, young. I come to check,
I come to stay with you,
and the Governor, & Father, & Simon, & the huddled men.

5

By the week we landed we were, most, used up.
Strange ships across us, after a fortnight's winds
unfavouring, frightened us;
bone-sad cold, sleet, scurvy; so were ill
many as one day we could have no sermons;
broils, quelled; a fatherless child-unkennelled; vermin
crowding & waiting: waiting.
And the day itself he leapt ashore young Henry Winthrop

6

(delivered from the waves; because he found
off their wigwams, sharp-eyed, a lone canoe
across a tidal river,
that water glittered fair & blue
& narrow, none of the other men could swim
and the plantation's prime theft up to him,
shouldered on a glad day
hard on the glorious feasting of thanksgiving) drowned.

7

How long with nothing in the ruinous heat,
clams & acorns stomaching, distinction perishing,
at which my heart rose,
with brackish water, we would sing.
When whispers knew the Governor's last bread
was browning in his oven, we were discourag'd.
The Lady Arbella dying—
dyings—at which my heart   rose, but I did submit.

8

That beyond the Atlantic wound our woes enlarge
is hard, hard that starvation burnishes our fear,
but I do gloss for You.
Strangers & pilgrims fare we here,
declaring we seek a City. Shall we be deceived?
I know whom I have trusted, & whom I have believed,
and that he is able to
keep   that I have committed to his charge.

9

Winter than summer worse, that first, like a file
on a quick, or the poison suck of a thrilled tooth;
and still we may unpack.
Wolves & storms among, uncouth
board-pieces, boxes, barrels vanish, grow
houses, rise. Motes that hop in sunlight slow
indoors, and I am Ruth
away: open my mouth, my eyes wet: I wóuld smile:

10

vellum I palm, and dream. Their forest dies
to greensward, privets, elms & towers, whence
a nightingale is throbbing.
Women sleep sound. I was happy once . .
(Something keeps on not happening; I shrink?)
These minutes all their passions & powers sink
and I am not one chance
for an unknown cry or a flicker of unknown eyes.

11

Chapped souls ours, by the day Spring's strong winds swelled,
Jack's pulpits arched, more glad. The shawl I pinned
flaps like a shooting soul
might in such weather Heaven send.
Succumbing half, in spirit, to a salmon sash
I prod the nerveless novel succotash—
I must be disciplined,
in arms, against that one, and our dissidents, and myself.

12

Versing, I shroud among the dynasties;
quarternion on quarternion, tireless I phrase
anything past, dead, far,
sacred, for a barbarous place.
—To please your wintry father? all this bald
abstract didactic rime I read appalled
harassed for your fame
mistress neither of fiery nor velvet verse, on your knees

13

hopeful & shamefast, chaste, laborious, odd,
whom the sea tore. —The damned roar with loss,
so they hug & are mean
with themselves, and I cannot be thus.
Why then do I repine, sick, bad, to long
after what must not be? I lie wrong
once more. For at fourteen
I found my heart more carnal and sitting loose from God,

14

vanity & the follies of youth took hold of me;
then the pox blasted, when the Lord returned.
That year for my sorry face
so-much-older Simon burned,
so Father smiled, with love. Their will be done.
He to me ill lingeringly, learning to shun
a bliss, a lightning blood
vouchsafed, what did seem life. I kissed his Mystery.

15

Drydust in God's eye the aquavivid skin
of Simon snoring lit with fountaining dawn
when my eyes unlid, sad.
John Cotton shines on Boston's sin—
I ám drawn, in pieties that seem
the weary drizzle of an unremembered dream.
Women have gone mad
at twenty-one. Ambition mines, atrocious, in.

16

Food endless, people few, all to be done.
As pippins roast, the question of the wolves
turns & turns.
Fangs of a wolf will keep, the neck
round of a child, that child brave. I remember who
in meeting smiled & was punisht, and I know who
whispered & was stockt.
We lead a thoughtful life. But Boston's cage we shun.

17

The winters close, Springs open, no child stirs
under my withering heart, O seasoned heart
God grudged his aid.
All things else soil like a shirt.
Simon is much away. My executive stales.
The town came through for the cartway by the pales,
but my patience is short.
I revolt from, I am like, these savage foresters

18

whose passionless dicker in the shade, whose glance
impassive & scant, belie their murderous cries
when quarry seems to show.
Again I must have been wrong, twice.
Unwell in a new way. Can that begin?
God brandishes. O love, O I love. Kin,
gather. My world is strange
and merciful, ingrown months, blessing a swelling trance.

19

So squeezed, wince you I scream? I love you & hate
off with you. Ages! *Useless.* Below my waist
he has me in Hell's vise.
Stalling. He let go. Come back: brace
me somewhere. No. No. Yes! everything down
hardens I press with horrible joy down
my back cracks like a wrist
shame I am voiding oh behind it is too late

20

hide me forever I work thrust I must free
now I all muscles & bones concentrate
what is living from dying?
Simon I must leave you so untidy
Monster you are killing me Be sure
I'll have you later Women do endure
I can *can* no longer
and it passes the wretched trap whelming and I am me

21

drencht & powerful. I did it with my body!
One proud tug greens Heaven. Marvellous,
unforbidding Majesty.
Swell, imperious bells. I fly.
Mountainous, woman not breaks and will bend:
sways God nearby: anguish comes to an end.
Blossomed Sarah, and I
blossom. Is that thing alive? I hear a famisht howl.

22

Beloved household, I am Simon's wife,
and the mother of Samuel—whom greedy yet I miss
out of his kicking place.
More in some ways I feel at a loss,
freer. Cantablanks & mummers, nears
longing for you. Our chopping scores my ears,
our costume bores my eyes.
St. George to the good sword, rise! chop-logic's rife

23

& fever & Satan & Satan's ancient fere.
Pioneering is not feeling well,
not Indians, beasts.
Not all their riddling can forestall
one leaving. Sam, your uncle has had to
go fróm us to live with God. 'Then Aunt went too?'
Dear, she does wait still.
Stricken: 'Oh. Then he takes   us one by one.' My dear.

24

Forswearing it otherwise, they starch their minds.
Folkmoots, & blether, blether. John Cotton rakes
to the synod of Cambridge.
Down from my body my legs flow,
out from it arms wave, on it my head shakes.
Now Mistress Hutchinson rings forth a call—
should she? many creep out at a broken wall—
affirming the Holy Ghost
dwells in one justified. Factioning passion blinds

25

all to all her good, all—can she be exiled?
Bitter sister, victim! I miss you.
—I miss you, Anne,
day or night weak as a child,
tender & empty, doomed, quick to no tryst.
—I hear you. Be kind, you who leaguer
my image in the mist.
—Be kind you, to one unchained eager far & wild

26

and if, O my love, my heart is breaking, please
neglect my cries and I will spare you. Deep
in Time's grave, Love's, you lie still.
Lie still. —Now? That happy shape
my forehead had under my most long, rare,
ravendark, hidden, soft bodiless hair
you award me still.
You must not love me, but   I do not bid you cease.

27

Veiled my eyes, attending. How can it be I?
Moist, with parted lips, I listen, wicked.
I shake in the morning & retch.
Brood I do on myself naked.
A fading world I dust, with fingers new.
—I have earned the right to be alone with you.
—What right can that be?
Convulsing, if you love, enough, like a sweet lie.

28

Not that, I know, you can. This cratered skin,
like the crabs & shells of my Palissy ewer, touch!
Oh, you do, you do?
Falls on me what I like a witch,
for lawless holds, annihilations of law
which Time and he and man abhor, foresaw:
sharper than what my Friend
brought me for my revolt when I moved smooth & thin,

29

faintings black, rigour, chilling, brown
parching, back, brain burning, the grey pocks
itch, a manic stench
of pustules snapping, pain floods the palm,
sleepless, or a red shaft with a dreadful start
rides at the chapel, like a slipping heart.
My soul strains in one qualm
ah but *this* is not to save me but to throw me down.

30

And out of this I lull. It lessens. Kiss me.
That once. As sings out up in sparkling dark
a trail of a star & dies,
while the breath flutters, sounding, mark,
so shorn ought such caresses to us be
who, deserving nothing, flush and flee
the darkness of that light,
a lurching frozen from a warm dream. Talk to me.

31

—it is Spring's New England. Pussy willows wedge
up in the wet. Milky crestings, fringed
yellow, in heaven, eyed
by the melting hand-in-hand or mere
desirers single, heavy-footed, rapt,
make surge poor human hearts. Venus is trapt—
the hefty pike shifts, sheer—
in Orion blazing. Warblings, odours, nudge to an edge—

32

—Ravishing, ha, what crouches outside ought,
flamboyant, ill, angelic. Often, now,
I am afraid of you.
I am a sobersides; I know.
I *want* to take you for my lover. —Do.
—I hear a madness. Harmless I to you
am not, not I? —No.
—I cannot but be. Sing a concord of our thought.

33
—Wan dolls in indigo on gold: refrain
my western lust. I am drowning in this past.
I lose sight of you
who mistress me from air. Unbraced
in delirium of the grand depths, giving away
haunters what kept me, I breathe solid spray.
—I am losing you!
Straiten me on. —I suffered living like a stain:

34
I trundle the bodies, on the iron bars,
over that fire backward & forth; they burn;
bits fall. I wonder if
I killed them. Women serve my turn.
—Dreams! You are good. —No. —Dense with hardihood
the wicked are dislodged, and lodged the good.
In green space we are safe.
God awaits us (but I   am yielding) who Hell wars.

35
—I cannot feel myself God waits. He flies
nearer a kindly world; or he is flown.
One Saturday's rescue
won't show. Man is entirely alone
may be. I am a man of griefs & fits
trying to be my friend. And the brown smock splits,
down the pale flesh a gash
broadens and Time holds up your heart against my eyes.

36
—Hard and divided heaven! creases me. Shame
is failing. My breath is scented, and I throw
hostile glances towards God.
Crumpling plunge of a pestle, bray:
sin cross & opposite, wherein I survive
nightmares of Eden. Reaches foul & live
he for me, this soul
to crunch, a minute tangle of eternal flame.

37
I fear Hell's hammer-wind. But fear does not wane.
Death's blossoms grain my hair; I cannot live.
A black joy clashes
joy, in twilight. The Devil said
'I will deal toward her softly, and her enchanting cries
will fool the horns of Adam.' Father of lies,
a male great pestle smashes
small women swarming towards the mortar's rim in vain.

38
I see the cruel spread Wings black with saints!
Silky my breasts not his, mine, mine, to withhold
or tender, tender.
I am sifting, nervous, and bold.
The light is changing. Surrender this loveliness
you cannot make me do. *But* I will. Yes.
What horror, down stormy air,
warps towards me? My threatening promise faints—

39

torture me, Father, lest not I be thine!
Tribunal terrible & pure, my God,
mercy for him and me.
Faces half-fanged, Christ drives abroad,
and though the crop hopes, Jane is so slipshod
I cry. Evil dissolves, & love, like foam;
that love. Prattle of children powers me home,
my heart claps like the swan's
under a frenzy of *who* love me & who shine.

40

As a canoe slides by on one strong stroke
hope his hélp not I, who do hardly bear
his gift still. But whisper
I am not utterly. I pare
an apple for my pipsqueak Mercy and
she runs & all need naked apples, fanned
their tinier envies.
Vomitings, trots, rashes. Can be hope a cloak?

41

for the man with cropt ears glares. My fingers tighten
my skirt. I pass. Alas! I pity all.
Shy, shy, with mé, Dorothy.
Moonrise, and frightening hoots. 'Mother,
how *long* will I be dead?' Our friend the owl
vanishes, darling, but your homing soul
retires on Heaven, Mercy:
not we one instant die, only our dark does lighten.

42

When by me in the dusk my child sits down
I am myself. Simon, if it's that loose,
let me wiggle it out.
You'll get a bigger one there, & bite.
How they loft, how their sizes delight and grate.
The proportioned, spiritless poems accumulate.
And they publish them
away in brutish London, for a hollow crown.

43

Father is not himself. He keeps his bed,
and threw a saffron scum Thursday. God-forsaken words
escaped him raving. Save,
Lord, thy servant zealous & just.
Sam he saw back from Harvard. He did scold
his secting enemies. His stomach is cold
while we drip, while
my baby John breaks out. O far from where he bred!

44

Bone of moaning: sung Where he has gone
a thousand summers by truth-hallowed souls;
be still. Agh, he is gone!
Where? I know. Beyond the shoal.
Still-all a Christian daughter grinds her teeth
a little. This our land has ghosted with
our dead: I am at home.
Finish, Lord, in me this work thou hast begun.

45

And they tower, whom the pear-tree lured
to let them fall, fierce mornings they reclined
down the brook-bank to the east
fishing for shiners with crookt pin,
wading, dams massing, well, and Sam's to be
a doctor in Boston. After the divisive sea,
and death's first feast,
and the galled effort on the wilderness endured,

46

Arminians, and the King bore against us;
of an 'inward light' we hear with horror.
Whose fan is in his hand
and he will thoroughly purge his floor,
come towards mé. I have what licks the joints
and bites the heart, which winter more appoints.
Iller I, oftener.
Hard at the outset; in the ending thus hard, thus?

47

Sacred & unutterable Mind
flashing thorough the universe one thought,
I do wait without peace.
In the article of death I budge.
Eat my sore breath, Black Angel. Let me die.
Body a-drain, when will you be dry
and countenance my speed
to Heaven's springs? lest stricter writhings have me declined.

48

'What are those pictures in the air at night,
Mother?' Mercy did ask. Space charged with faces
day & night! I place
a goatskin's fetor, and sweat: fold me
in savoury arms. Something is shaking, wrong.
He smells the musket and lifts it. It is long.
It points at my heart.
Missed he must have. In the gross storm of sunlight

49

I sniff a fire burning without outlet,
consuming acrid its own smoke. It's me.
Ruined laughter sounds
outside. Ah but I waken, free.
And so I am about again. I hagged
a fury at the short maid, whom tongues tagged,
and I am sorry. Once
less I was anxious when more passioned to upset

50

the mansion & the garden & the beauty of God.
Insectile unreflective busyness
blunts & does amend.
Hangnails, piles, fibs, life's also.
But we are that from which draws back a thumb.
The seasons stream and, somehow, I am become
an old woman. It's so:
I look. I bear to look. Strokes once more his rod.

51

My window gives on the graves, in our great new house
(how many burned?) upstairs, among the elms.
I lie, & endure, & wonder.
A haze slips sometimes over my dreams
and holiness on horses' bells shall stand.
Wandering pacemaker, unsteadying friend,
in a redskin calm I wait:
beat when you will our end. Sinkings & droopings drowse.

52

They say thro' the fading winter Dorothy fails,
my second, who than I bore one more, nine;
and I see her inearthed. I linger.
Seaborn she wed knelt before Simon;
Simon I, and linger. Black-yellow seething, vast
it lies fróm me, mine: all they look aghast.
It will be a glorious arm.
Docile I watch. My wreckt chest hurts when Simon pales.

53

In the yellowing days your faces wholly fail,
at Fall's onset. Solemn voices fade.
I feel no coverlet.
Light notes leap, a beckon, swaying
the titled, sickening ear within. I'll—I'll—
I am closed & coming. Somewhere! I defile
wide as a cloud, in a cloud,
unfit, desirous, glad—even the singings veil—

54

—You are not ready? You áre ready. Pass,
as shadow gathers shadow in the welling night.
Fireflies of childhood torch
you down. We commit our sister down.
One candle mourn by, which a lover gave,
the use's edge and order of her grave.
Quiet? Moisture shoots.
Hungry throngs collect. They sword into the carcass.

55

Headstones stagger under great draughts of time
after heads pass out, and their world must reel
speechless, blind in the end
about its chilling star: thrift tuft,
whin cushion—nothing. Already with the wounded flying
dark air fills, I am a closet of secrets dying,
races murder, foxholes hold men,
reactor piles wage slow upon the wet brain rime.

56

I must pretend to leave you. Only you draw off
a benevolent phantom. I say you seem to me
drowned towns off England,
featureless as those myriads
who what bequeathed save fire-ash, fossils, burled
in the open river-drifts of the Old World?
Simon lived on for years.
I renounce not even ragged glances, small teeth, nothing,

57

O all your ages at the mercy of my loves
together lie at once, forever or
so long as I happen.
In the rain of pain & departure, still
Love has no body and presides the sun,
and elfs from silence melody. I run.
Hover, utter, still,
a sourcing   whom my lost candle like the firefly loves.

NOTES

    1–4 The poem is about the woman but this exordium is spoken by the poet, his voice modulating in stanza 4, line 8 [4.8] into hers.

    1.1 He was not Governor until after her death.

    1.5 Sylvester (the translator of Du Bartas) and Quarles, her favourite poets; unfortunately.

  5.4, 5 Many details are from quotations in Helen Campbell's biography, the Winthrop papers, narratives, town histories.

  8.4ff. Scriptural passages are sometimes ones she used herself, as this in her *Meditation liii*.

   11.8 *that one*: the Old One.

12.5–13.2 The poet interrupts.

   18.7 Her first child was not born until about 1633.

   22.6 *chopping*: disputing, snapping, haggling; axing.

   23.1 *fere*: his friend Death.

   24.1 Her irony of 22.8 intensifies.

   24.2 *rakes*: inclines, as a mast; bows.

   25.3 One might say: He is enabled to speak, at last, in the fortune of an echo of her—and when she is loneliest (her former spiritual adviser having deserted Anne Hutchinson, and this her closest friend banished), as if she had summoned him; and only thus, perhaps, is she enabled to hear him.

This second section of the poem is a dialogue, his voice however ceasing well before it ends at 39.4, and hers continuing for the whole third part, until the coda (54–57).

29.1–4 Cf. Isa. 1:5.

29.5, 6 After a Klee.

33.1 Cf., on Byzantine icons, Frederick Rolfe ('Baron Corvo'): 'Who ever dreams of praying (with expectation of response) for the prayer of a Tintoretto or a Titian, or a Bellini, or a Botticelli? But who can refrain from crying "O Mother!" to these unruffleable wan dolls in indigo on gold?' (quoted from *The Desire and Pursuit of the Whole* by Graham Greene in *The Lost Childhood*).

33.5, 6 'Délires des grandes profondeurs,' described by Cousteau and others; a euphoria, sometimes fatal, in which the hallucinated diver offers passing fish his line, helmet, anything.

35.3, 4 As of cliffhangers, movie serials wherein each week's episode ends with a train bearing down on the strapped heroine or with the hero dangling over an abyss into which Indians above him peer with satisfaction before they hatchet the rope. *rescue*: forcible recovery (by the owner) of good distrained.

37.7, 8 After an engraving somewhere in Fuchs's collections. *Bray*, above (36.4), puns.

39.5 The stanza is unsettled, like 24, by a middle line, signaling a broad transition.

42.8 *brutish*: her epithet for London in a kindly passage about the Great Fire.

46.1, 2 Arminians, rebels against the doctrine of unconditional election. Her husband alone opposed the law condemning Quakers to death.

46.3, 4 Matthew 3:12.

46.5, 6 Rheumatic fever, after a celebrated French description.

48.2ff. *Space . . . outside*: delirium.

51.5 Cf. Zech. 14:20.

51.6 *Wandering pacemaker*: a disease of the heart, here the heart itself.

52.4 Seaborn Cotton, John's eldest son; Bradstreet being then magistrate.

52.5, 6 Dropsical, a complication of the last three years. Line 7 she actually said.

55.4 *thrift*: the plant, also called Our Lady's cushion.

55.8 *wet brain*: edema.

56.5, 6 Cf. G. R. Levy, *The Gate of Horn*, p. 5.

FROM

His Thought Made Pockets &
The Plane Buckt

(1958)

They Have

A thing O say a sixteenth of an inch
long, with whiskers
& wings it doesn't use, & many legs,
has all this while been wandering in a tiny space
on the black wood table by my burning chair.
I see it has a feeler of some length
it puts out before it.
That must be how it was following the circuit
of the bottom of my wine-glass, vertical: Mâcon: I thought
it smelt & wanted some but couldn't get hold.
Now here's another thing, on my paper, a fluff
of legs, and I blow: my brothers & sisters go away.
But here he's back, & got between the pad
& padback, where I save him and
shift him to my blue shirt, where he is.
The other little one's gone somewhere else.
They have things easy.

The Poet's Final Instructions

Dog-tired, suisired, will now my body down
near Cedar Avenue in Minneap,
when my crime comes. I am blazing with hope.
Do me glory, come the whole way across town.

I couldn't rest from hell just anywhere,
in commonplaces. Choiring & strange my pall!
I might not lie still in the waste of St Paul
or buy D A D ' S root beer; good signs I forgive.

Drop here, with honour due, my trunk & brain
among the passioning of my countrymen
unable to read, rich, proud of their tags
and proud of me. Assemble all my bags!
Bury me in a hole, and give a cheer,
near Cedar on Lake Street, where the used cars live.

from *The Black Book (iii)*

Lover & child, a little sing.
From long-lockt cattle-cars who grope
Who near a place of showers come
Foul no more, whose murmuring
Grows in a hiss of gas will clear them home:
Away from & toward me: a little soap,
Disrobing, *Achtung!* in a dirty hope,
They shuffle with their haircuts in to die.
Lift them an elegy, poor you and I,
Fair & strengthless as seafoam
Under a deserted sky.

A Sympathy, A Welcome

Feel for your bad fall how could I fail,
poor Paul, who had it so good.
I can offer you only: this world like a knife.
Yet you'll get to know your mother
and humourless as you do look you will laugh
and all the others
will NOT be fierce to you, and loverhood
will swing your soul like a broken bell
deep in a forsaken wood, poor Paul,
whose wild bad father loves you well.

Mr. Pou & the Alphabet

(1961)

Mr. Pou & the Alphabet—
which he do not like

A is for *awful*, which things are;
B is for *bear* them, well as we can.
C is for *can* we? D is for *dare*:
E is for *each* dares, being a man.
(What does a man do? bears and dares;
and how does a little boy fare? He fares.)
F is for *floor* we stamp wif our foot,
G is for *grimy* we getting from play,
H is for *Hell* wherein they do put
the bad guys, maybe. Oh, and I is for *'Ay'*
(And this will puzzle the Little Pou,
but his mommy can explain it. Do.)
J is for *Jackknife* which later will come,
when Poukie is bigger, K is for *key*.
L is for *Little* Pou, M is for some
men who have definite reason to be.
And N is for *now*, the best time of all,
And O is for *ouch* when it hurts—quite so.
P is for *Poukie*, of Paul and *piano*,
and Q is for *quiet*, while Mommy tells Paul.
R is for *rudiments* Poukie now learn.
S is for *sea-horse*, erect fish, weird,
T is for *Turks* whom we take by the beard.
U is for *utter*-don't-know-where-to turn.
V is for *vowels* the Pou is to learn.
(So vivid splendid subjects hide ahead,
the stars, the grasses, asses and wisemen, letters and the word.)
W's for *why*, which ask and ask;
X is for *Xmas*, where I cannot be.

Y is for *Yes* (do his Daddy love he?)
Z is for *zig-zag*—a part of our task.
(Straight's better, but few can.
My Xmas hope: boy head for man.)

FROM

The Dream Songs

(1969)

I

Huffy Henry hid   the day,
unappeasable Henry sulked.
I see his point,—a trying to put things over.
It was the thought that they thought
They could *do* it made Henry wicked & away.
But he should have come out and talked.

All the world like a woolen lover
once did seem on Henry's side.
Then came a departure.
Thereafter nothing fell out as it might or ought.
I don't see how Henry, pried
open for all the world to see, survived.

What he has now to say is a long
wonder the world can bear & be.
Once in a sycamore I was glad
all at the top, and I sang.
Hard on the land wears the strong sea
and empty grows every bed.

3
A Stimulant for an Old Beast

Acacia, burnt myrrh, velvet, pricky stings.
—I'm not so young but not so very old,
said screwed-up lovely 23.
A final sense of being right out in the cold,
unkissed.
(—My psychiatrist can lick your psychiatrist.) Women get under
things.

All these old criminals sooner or later
have had it. I've been reading old journals.
Gottwald & Co., out of business now.
Thick chests quit. Double agent, Joe.
She holds her breath like a seal
and is white & smoother.

Rilke was a *jerk*.
I admit his griefs & music
& titled spelled all-disappointed ladies.
A threshold worse than the circles
where the vile settle & lurk,
Rilke's. As I said,—

4

Filling her compact & delicious body
with chicken páprika, she glanced at me
twice.
Fainting with interest, I hungered back
and only the fact of her husband & four other people
kept me from springing on her

or falling at her little feet and crying
'You are the hottest one for years of night
Henry's dazed eyes
have enjoyed, Brilliance.' I advanced upon
(despairing) my spumoni. —Sir Bones: is stuffed,
de world, wif feeding girls.

—Black hair, complexion Latin, jewelled eyes
downcast . . . The slob beside her   feasts . . . What wonders is
she sitting on, over there?
The restaurant buzzes. She might as well be on Mars.
Where did it all go wrong? There ought to be a law against Henry.
—Mr. Bones: there is.

8

The weather was fine. They took away his teeth,
white & helpful; bothered his backhand;
halved his green hair.
They blew out his loves, his interests. 'Underneath,'
(they called in iron voices) 'understand,
is nothing. So there.'

The weather was very fine. They lifted off
his covers till he showed, and cringed & pled
to see himself less.
They installed mirrors till he flowed. 'Enough'
(murmured they) 'if you will watch Us instead,
yet you may saved be. Yes.'

The weather fleured. They weakened all his eyes,
and burning thumbs into his ears, and shook
his hand like a notch.
They flung long silent speeches. (Off the hook!)
They sandpapered his plumpest hope. (So capsize.)
They took away his crotch.

14

Life, friends, is boring. We must not say so.
After all, the sky flashes, the great sea yearns,
we ourselves flash and yearn,
and moreover my mother told me as a boy
(repeatingly) 'Ever to confess you're bored
means you have no

Inner Resources.' I conclude now I have no
inner resources, because I am heavy bored.
Peoples bore me,
literature bores me, especially great literature,
Henry bores me, with his plights & gripes
as bad as achilles,

who loves people and valiant art, which bores me.
And the tranquil hills, & gin, look like a drag
and somehow a dog
has taken itself & its tail considerably away
into mountains or sea or sky, leaving
behind: me, wag.

26

The glories of the world struck me, made me aria, once.
—What happen then, Mr Bones?
if be you cares to say.
—Henry. Henry became interested in women's bodies,
his loins were & were the   scene of stupendous achievement.
Stupor. Knees, dear. Pray.

All the knobs & softnesses of, my God,
the ducking & trouble it swarm on Henry,
at one time.
—What happen then, Mr Bones?
you seems excited-like.
—Fell Henry back into   the original crime: art, rime

besides a sense of others, my God, my God,
and a jealousy for the honour (alive) of his country,
what can get more odd?
and discontent with the thriving gangs & pride.
—What happen then, Mr Bones?
—I had a most marvellous   piece of luck. I died.

There sat down, once, a thing on Henry's heart
só heavy, if he had a hundred years
& more, & weeping, sleepless, in all them time
Henry could not make good.
Starts again always in Henry's ears
the little cough somewhere, an odour, a chime.

And there is another thing he has in mind
like a grave Sienese face a thousand years
would fail to blur the still profiled reproach of. Ghastly,
with open eyes, he attends, blind.
All the bells say: too late. This is not for tears;
thinking.

But never did Henry, as he thought he did,
end anyone and hacks her body up
and hide the pieces, where they may be found.
He knows: he went over everyone, & nobody's missing.
Often he reckons, in the dawn, them up.
Nobody is ever missing.

40

I'm scared a lonely. Never see my son,
easy be not to see anyone,
combers out to sea
know they're goin somewhere but not me.
Got a little poison, got a little gun,
I'm scared a lonely.

I'm scared a only one thing, which is me,
from othering I don't take nothin, see,
for any hound dog's sake.
But this is where I livin, where I rake
my leaves and cop my promise, this' where we
cry oursel's awake.

Wishin was dyin but I gotta make
it all this way to that bed on these feet
where peoples said to meet.
Maybe but even if I see my son
forever never, get back on the take,
free, black & forty-one.

63

Bats have no bankers and they do not drink
and cannot be arrested and pay no tax
and, in general, bats have it made.
Henry for joining the human race is *bats*,
known to be so, by few them who think,
out of the cave.

Instead of the cave! ah lovely-chilly, dark,
ur-moist his cousins hang in hundreds or swerve
with personal radar,
crisisless, kid. Instead of the cave? I serve,
inside, my blind term. Filthy four-foot lights
reflect on the whites of our eyes.

He then salutes for sixty years of it
just now a one of valor and insights,
a theatrical man,
O scholar & Legionnaire who as quickly might
have killed as cast you. *Olè*. Stormed with years
he tranquil commands and appears.

68

I heard, could be, a Hey there from the wing,
and I went on: Miss Bessie soundin good
that one, that night of all,
I feelin fair mysef, taxes & things
seem to be back in line, like everybody should
and nobody in the snow on call

so, as I say, the house is givin hell
to *Yellow Dog*, I blowin like it too
and Bessie always do
when she make a very big sound—after, well,
no sound—I see she totterin—I cross which stage
even at Henry's age

in 2–3 seconds: then we wait and see.
I hear strange horns, Pinetop he hit some chords,
Charlie start *Empty Bed*,
they all come hangin Christmas on some tree
after trees thrown out—sick-house's white birds',
black to the birds instead.

69

Love her he doesn't but the thought he puts
into that young woman
would launch a national product
complete with TV spots & skywriting
outlets in Bonn & Tokyo
I mean it

Let it be known that nine words have not passed
between herself and Henry;
looks, smiles.
God help Henry, who deserves it all
every least part of that infernal & unconscious
woman, and the pain.

I feel as if, unique, she . . . Biddable?
Fates, conspire.
—Mr Bones, *please.*
—Vouchsafe me, Sleepless One,
a personal experience of the body of Mrs Boogry
before I pass from lust!

76
Henry's Confession

Nothin very bad happen to me lately.
How you explain that? —I explain that, Mr Bones,
terms o' your bafflin odd sobriety.
Sober as man can get, no girls, no telephones,
what could happen bad to Mr Bones?
—*If* life is a handkerchief sandwich,

in a modesty of death I join my father
who dared so long agone leave me.
A bullet on a concrete stoop
close by a smothering southern sea
spreadeagled on an island, by my knee.
—You is from hunger, Mr Bones,

I offers you this handkerchief, now set
your left foot by my right foot,
shoulder to shoulder, all that jazz,
arm in arm, by the beautiful sea,
hum a little, Mr Bones.
—I saw nobody coming, so I went instead.

101

A shallow lake, with many waterbirds,
especially egrets: I was showing Mother around,
An extraordinary vivid dream
of Betty & Douglas, and Don—his mother's estate
was on the grounds of a lunatic asylum.
He showed me around.

A policeman trundled a siren up the walk.
It was 6:05 p.m., Don was late home.
I askt if he ever saw
the inmates—'No, they never leave their cells.'
Betty was downstairs, Don called down 'A drink'
while showering.

I can't go into the meaning of the dream
except to say a sense of total LOSS
afflicted me thereof:
an absolute disappearance of continuity & love
and children away at school, the weight of the cross,
and everything is what it seems.

It was the blue & plain ones. I forgot all that.
My own clouds darkening hung.
Besides, it wasn't serious.
They took them in different rooms & fed them lies.
'She admitted you wanted to get rid of it.'
'He told us he told you to.'

The Force, with its rapists con-men murderers,
has been our Pride (trust Henry) eighty years;—
now Teddy was hard on.
Still the tradition persists, beat up, beat on,
take, take. Frame. Get set; cover up.
The Saturday confessions are really something.

Here was there less or nothing in question but horror.
She left his brother's son two minutes but—
as I say I forget that—
during the time he drowned. The laundry lived
and they lived, uncharged, and went their ways apart
with the blessing of the N.Y. Police Force.

The animal moment, when   he sorted out her tail
in a rump session with the vivid hostess
whose guests had finally gone,
was stronger, though so limited, though failed
all normal impulse before her interdiction, yes,
and Henry gave in.

I'd like to have your baby, but, she moaned,
I'm married. Henry muttered to himself
So am I and was glad
to keep chaste. If this lady he had had
scarcely could he have have ever forgiven himself
and how would he have atoned?

—Mr Bones, you strong on moral these days, hey?
It's good to be faithful but it ain't natural,
as you knows.
—I knew what I knew when I knew when I was astray,
all those bright painful years, forgiving all
but when Henry & his wives came to blows.

—That's enough of that, Mr Bones. *Some* lady you make.
Honour the burnt cork, be a vaudeville man,
I'll sing you now a song
the like of whích may bring your heart to break:
he's gone! and we don't know where. When he began
taking the pistol out & along,

you was just a little; but gross fears
accompanied us along the beaches, pal.
My mother was scared almost to death.
He was going to swim out, with me, forevers,
and a swimmer strong he was in the phosphorescent   Gulf,
but he decided on lead.

That mad drive wiped out my childhood. I put him down
while all the same on forty years I love him
stashed in Oklahoma
besides his brother Will. Bite the nerve of the town
for anyone so desperate. I repeat: I love him
until *I* fall into coma.

153

I'm cross with god who has wrecked this generation.
First he seized Ted, then Richard, Randall, and now Delmore.
In between he gorged on Sylvia Plath.
That was a first rate haul. He left alive
fools I could number like a kitchen knife
but Lowell he did not touch.

Somewhere the enterprise continues, not—
yellow the sun lies on the baby's blouse—
in Henry's staggered thought.
I suppose the word would be, we must submit.
Later.
I hang, and I will not be part of it.

A friend of Henry's contrasted God's career
with Mozart's, leaving Henry with nothing to say
but praise for a word so apt.
We suffer on, a day, a day, a day.
And never again can come, like a man slapped,
news like this

Am tame now. You may touch me, who had thrilled
(before) your tips, twitcht from your breast your heart,
& burnt your willing brain.
I am tame now. Undead, I was not killed
by Henry's viewers but maimed. It is my art
to buzz the spotlight in vain,

flighting 'at random' while Addison wins.
I would not war with Addison. I love him
and Addison so loves me back
me backsides, I may perish in his grins
& grip. I would he liked me less, less grim.
But he has helpt me, slack

& sick & hopeful, anew to know what man—
scrubbing the multiverse with dazzled thought—
still has in store for man:
a doghouse or a cave, is all we could,
according to my dreams. I stand in doubt,
surrounded by holy wood.

233
Cantatrice

Misunderstanding. Misunderstanding, misunderstanding.
Are we stationed here among another thing?
Sometimes I wonder.
After the lightning, this afternoon, came thunder:
the natural world makes sense: cats hate water
and love fish.

Fish, plankton, bats' radar, the sense of fish
who glide up the coast of South America
and head for Gibraltar.
How do they know it's there? We call this *instinct*
by which we dream we know what instinct is,
like misunderstanding.

I was soft on a green girl once and we smiled across
and married, childed. Never did we truly take in
one burning wing.
Henry flounders. What is the name of that fish?
So better organized than we are oh.
Sing to me that name, enchanter, sing!

308
An Instructions to Critics

The women of Kilkenny weep when the team loses,
they don't see the match but they cry. Mad bettors everywhere,
the sign "Turf Accountant",
men slipping in & out. People are all the same,
the seaman argued: Henry feels the Spanish & Irish
& Bengalis are thoroughly odd.

Americans, whom I prefer, are hopelessly normal.
The Japanese are barely comprehensible & formal,
formal Henry found.
We should have lowered the boom
on ourselves in our mother's womb,
dixit Henry's pal above ground.

My baby chatters. I feel the end is near
& strong of my large work, which will appear,
and baffle everybody.
They'll seek the strange soul, in rain & mist,
whereas they should recall the pretty cousins they kissed,
and stick with the sweet switch of the body.

Famisht Henry ate everything in sight
after his ancient fast. His fasting was voluntary,
self-imposed.
He specially liked hunks of decent bread
sopped in olive-oil & cut raw onion,
specially.

Hunger was constitutional with him,
women, cigarettes, liquor, need need need
until he went to pieces.
The pieces sat up & wrote. They did not heed
their piecedom but kept very quietly on
among the chaos.

An old old mistress recently rang up,
here in Ireland, to see how Henry was:
how was he? delighted!
He thought she was 3000 miles away,
safe with her children in New York: she's coming at five:
we'll wélcome her!

385

My daughter's heavier. Light leaves are flying.
Everywhere in enormous numbers turkeys will be dying
and other birds, all their wings.
They never greatly flew. Did they wish to?
I should know. Off away somewhere once I knew
such things.

Or good Ralph Hodgson back then did, or does.
The man is dead whom Eliot praised. My praise
follows and flows too late.
Fall is grievy, brisk. Tears behind the eyes
almost fall. Fall comes to us as a prize
to rouse us toward our fate.

My house is made of wood and it's made well,
unlike us. My house is older than Henry;
that's fairly old.
If there were a middle   ground between things and the soul
or if the sky resembled more the sea,
I wouldn't have to scold

my heavy daughter.

Love & Fame

(1970)

Cadenza on Garnette

'If I had said out passions as they were,'
plain-saying Wordsworth confided down deep age,
'the poems could never have been published.'
Ha! a confrère.

She set up a dazing clamour across this blood
in one of Brooks Hall's little visiting rooms.
In blunt view of whoever might pass by
we fondled each other's wonders.

One night she couldn't come down, she had a cold,
so I took away a talkative friend of hers,
to squirrel together inklings as to Garnette,
any, no matter what, she did, said, was.

O it flowed fuller than the girl herself,
I feasted on Louise.
I all but fell in love with her instead,
so rich with news.

Allen long after, being taxed obscenely
in a news-sheet of Spoleto, international town,
complained to me next day: His aim was tell it all.
Poets! . . Lovers & secrets!

How did we break off, now I come to it,
I puzzle. Did she date somebody else
& I warred with that & she snapped 'You don't own me'
or did the flare just little by little fall?

so that I cut in & was cut in on,
the travelling spotlights coloured, the orchestra gay,
without emphasis finally,
pressing each other's hand as he took over.

Images of Elspeth

O when I grunted, over lines and her,
my Muse a nymphet & my girl with men
older, of money, continually
lawyers & so, myself a flat-broke Junior.

But the one who made me wild
was who she let take naked photographs
never she showed me but she was proud of.
Unnerving; dire.

My love confused confused with after loves
not ever over time did I outgrow.
Solemn, alone my Muse grew taller.
Rejection slips developed signatures,

many thought Berryman was under weigh,
he wasn't sure himself.
Elspeth became two snapshots in his keeping,
with all her damned clothes on.

She married a Law School dean & flourisheth.
I almost married, with four languages
a ballerina in London, and I should have done.
—Drawing the curtain over fragrant scenes

& interviews malodorous, find me
domestic with my Muse
who had manifested, well, a sense of humour
fatal to bardic pretension.

Dance! from Savannah Garnette with your slur
hypnotic, you'll stay many.
I walked forth to a cold snow to post letters
to a foreign editor & a West Coast critic

wishing I could lay my old hands somewhere on those snapshots.

Two Organs

I remind myself at that time of Plato's uterus—
of the seven really good courses I ever took
one was a seminar with Edman met at night
in his apartment, where we read them all

all the Dialogues, in chronological order, through
so that I got *something* out of Columbia—
Plato's uterus, I say,
an animal passionately longing for children

and, if long unsatisfied after puberty,
prone to range angrily, blocking the air passages
& causing distress & disease.
For 'children' read: big fat fresh original & characteristic poems.

My longing yes was a woman's
She can't know can she *what kind* of a baby
she's going with all the will in the world to produce?
I suffered trouble over this,

I didn't want my next poem to be *exactly* like Yeats
or exactly like Auden
since in that case where the hell was *I*?
but what instead *did* I want it to sound like?

I couldn't sleep at night, I attribute my life-long insomnia
to my uterine struggles. 'You must undress'
a young poet writes to me from Oregon
'the great face of the body.'

The Isolation so, young & now I find older,
American, & other.
While the rest of England was strolling thro' the Crystal Palace
Arnold was gnashing his teeth on a mountain in Sicily.

An eccentric friend, a Renaissance scholar, sixty-odd,
unworldly, he writes limericks in Medieval Latin,
stood up in the rowboat fishing to take a leak
& exclaimed as he was about it with excitement

'I wish my penis was big enough for this whole lake!'
My phantasy precisely at twenty:
to satisfy at once all Barnard & Smith
& have enough left over for Miss Gibbs's girls.

Olympus

In my serpentine researches
I came on a book review in *Poetry*
which began, with sublime assurance,
a comprehensive air of majesty,

'The art of poetry
is amply distinguished from the manufacture of verse
by the animating presence in the poetry
of a fresh idiom: language

so twisted & posed in a form
that it not only expresses the matter in hand
but adds to the stock of available reality.'
I was never altogether the same man after *that*.

I found this new Law-giver all unknown
except in the back numbers of a Cambridge quarterly
Hound & Horn, just defunct.
I haunted on Sixth Avenue until

at 15¢ apiece or 25
I had all 28 numbers
& had fired my followers at Philolexian & Boar's Head
with the merits of this prophet.

My girls suffered during this month or so,
so did my seminars & lectures &
my poetry even. To be a *critic*, ah,
how deeper & more scientific.

I wrote & printed an essay on Yeats's plays
re-deploying all of Blackmur's key terms
& even his sentence-structure wherever I could.
When he answered by hand from Boston my nervous invitation

to come & be honoured at our annual Poetry Reading,
it must have been ten minutes before I could open the envelope.
I got *him* to review Tate's book of essays
& *Mark* to review *The Double Agent*. Olympus!

I have travelled in some high company since
but never so dizzily.
I have had some rare girls since but never one so philosophical
as that same Spring (my last Spring there) Jean Bennett.

Message

Amplitude,—voltage,—the one friend calls for the one,
the other for the other, in my work;
in verse & prose. Well, hell.
I am not writing an autobiography-in-verse, my friends.

Impressions, structures, tales, from Columbia in the Thirties
& the Michaelmas term at Cambridge in '36,
followed by some later. It's not my life.
That's occluded & lost.

That consisted of lectures on St Paul,
scrimmages with women, singular moments
of getting certain things absolutely right.
Laziness, liquor, bad dreams.

That consisted of three wives & many friends,
whims & emergencies, discoveries, losses.
It's been a long trip. Would I make it again?
But once a Polish belle bared me out & was kind to it.

I don't remember why I sent this message.
Children! children! form the point of all.
Children & high art.
Money in the bank is also something.

We will all die, & the evidence
is: Nothing after that.
Honey, we don't rejoin.
The thing meanwhile, I suppose, is to be courageous & kind.

Damned

Damned. Lost & *damned*. And I find I'm pregnant.
It must have been in a shuffle of disrobing
or shortly after.
I confess: I don't know what to do.

She wept steadily all thro' the performance.
As soon as I tucked it in she burst into tears.
She had a small mustache but was otherwise gifted,
riding, & crying her heart out.

(She had been married two years) I was amazed.
(Her first adultery) I was scared & guilty.
I said 'What are you crying for, darling? *Don't.*'
She stuttered something & wept on.

She came again & again, twice ejecting me
over her heaving. I turned my head aside
to avoid her goddamned tears,
getting in my beard.

I am busy tired mad lonely & old.
O this has been a long long night of wrest.

I saw her once again: on a busy sidewalk
outside a grocery store
& she was big & I did *not* say 'Is it mine?'
I congratulated her.

Brighter it waxeth; it's almost seven.

Despair

It seems to be DARK all the time.
I have difficulty walking.
I can remember what to say to my seminar
but I don't know that I want to.

I said in a Song once: I am unusually tired.
I repeat that & increase it.
I'm vomiting.
I broke down today in the slow movement of K.365.

I certainly don't think I'll last much longer.
I wrote: 'There may be horribles.'
I increase that.
(I think she took her little breasts away.)

I am in love with my excellent baby.
Crackles! in darkness HOPE; & disappears.
Lost arts.
Vanishings.

Walt! We're downstairs,
even you don't comfort me
but I join your risk my dear friend & go with you.
There are no matches

Utter, His Father, one word

Eleven Addresses to the Lord

I

Master of beauty, craftsman of the snowflake,
inimitable contriver,
endower of Earth so gorgeous & different from the boring Moon,
thank you for such as it is my gift.

I have made up a morning prayer to you
containing with precision everything that most matters.
'According to Thy will' the thing begins.
It took me off & on two days. It does not aim at eloquence.

You have come to my rescue again & again
in my impassable, sometimes despairing years.
You have allowed my brilliant friends to destroy themselves
and I am still here, severely damaged, but functioning.

Unknowable, as I am unknown to my guinea pigs:
how can I 'love' you?
I only as far as gratitude & awe
confidently & absolutely go.

I have no idea whether we live again.
It doesn't seem likely
from either the scientific or the philosophical point of view
but certainly all things are possible to you,

and I believe as fixedly in the Resurrection-appearances to Peter
                        & to Paul
as I believe I sit in this blue chair.
Only that may have been a special case
to establish their initiatory faith.

Whatever your end may be, accept my amazement.
May I stand until death forever at attention
for any your least instruction or enlightenment.
I even feel sure you will assist me again, Master of insight &

beauty.

2

Holy, as I suppose I dare to call you
without pretending to know anything about you
but infinite capacity everywhere & always
& in particular certain goodness to me.

Yours is the crumpling, to my sister-in-law terrifying thunder,
yours the candelabra buds sticky in Spring,
Christ's mercy,
the gloomy wisdom of godless Freud:

yours the lost souls in ill-attended wards,
those agonized thro' the world
at this instant of time, all evil men,
Belsen, Omaha Beach,—

incomprehensible to man your ways.
May be the Devil after all exists.
'I don't try to reconcile anything' said the poet at eighty,
'This is a damned strange world.'

Man is ruining the pleasant earth & man.
What at last, my Lord, will you allow?
Postpone till after my children's deaths your doom
if it be thy ineffable, inevitable will.

I say 'Thy kingdom come', it means nothing to me.
Hast Thou prepared astonishments for man?
One sudden Coming? Many so believe.
So not, without knowing anything, do I.

3

Sole watchman of the flying stars, guard me
against my flicker of impulse lust: teach me
to see them as sisters & daughters. Sustain
my grand endeavours: husbandship & crafting.

Forsake me not when my wild hours come;
grant me sleep nightly, grace soften my dreams;
achieve in me patience till the thing be done,
a careful view of my achievement come.

Make me from time to time the gift of the shoulder.
When all hurt nerves whine shut away the whiskey.
Empty my heart toward Thee.
Let me pace without fear the common path of death.

Cross am I sometimes with my little daughter:
fill her eyes with tears. Forgive me, Lord.
Unite my various soul,
sole watchman of the wide & single stars.

4

If I say Thy name, art Thou there? It may be so.
Thou art not absent-minded, as I am.
I am so much so I had to give up driving.
You attend, I feel, to the matters of man.

Across the ages certain blessings swarm,
horrors accumulate, the best men fail:
Socrates, Lincoln, Christ mysterious.
Who can search Thee out?

except Isaiah & Pascal, who saw.
I dare not ask that vision, though a piece of it
at last in crisis was vouchsafèd me.
I altered then for good, to become yours.

Caretaker! take care, for we run in straits.
Daily, by night, we walk naked to storm,
some threat of wholesale loss, to ruinous fear.
Gift us with long cloaks & adrenalin.

Who haunt the avenues of Angkor Wat
recalling all that prayer, that glory dispersed,
haunt me at the corner of Fifth & Hennepin.
Shield & fresh fountain! Manifester! Even mine.

5

Holy, & holy. The damned are said to say
'We never thought we would come into this place.'
I'm fairly clear, my Friend, there's no such place
ordained for inappropriate & evil man.

Surely they fall dull, & forget. We too,
the more or less just, I feel fall asleep
dreamless forever while the worlds hurl out.
Rest may be your ultimate gift.

Rest or transfiguration! come & come
whenever Thou wilt. My daughter & my son
fend will without me, when my work is done
in Your opinion.

Strengthen my widow, let her dream on me
thro' tranquil hours less & down to less.
Abrupt elsewhere her heart, I sharply hope.
I leave her in wise Hands.

6

Under new management, Your Majesty:
Thine. I have solo'd mine since childhood, since
my father's suicide when I was twelve
blew out my most bright candle faith, and look at me.

I served at Mass six dawns a week from five,
adoring Father Boniface & you,
memorizing the Latin he explained.
Mostly we worked alone. One or two women.

Then my poor father frantic. Confusions & afflictions
followed my days. Wives left me.
Bankrupt I closed my doors. You pierced the roof
twice & again. Finally you opened my eyes.

My double nature fused in that point of time
three weeks ago day before yesterday.
Now, brooding thro' a history of the early Church,
I identify with everybody, even the heresiarchs.

7
After a Stoic, a Peripatetic, a Pythagorean,
Justin Martyr studied the words of the Saviour,
finding them short, precise, terrible, & full of refreshment.
I am tickled to learn this.

Let one day desolate Sherry, fair, thin, tall,
at 29 today her life the Sahara Desert,
who has never once enjoyed a significant relation,
so find His lightning words.

8

A PRAYER FOR THE SELF

Who am I worthless that You spent such pains
and take may pains again?
I do not understand; but I believe.
Jonquils respond with wit to the teasing breeze.

Induct me down my secrets. Stiffen this heart
to stand their horrifying cries, O cushion
the first the second shocks, will to a halt
in mid-air there demons who would be at me.

May fade before, sweet morning on sweet morning,
I wake my dreams, my fan-mail go astray,
and do me little goods I have not thought of,
ingenious & beneficial Father.

Ease in their passing my beloved friends,
all others too I have cared for in a travelling life,
anyone anywhere indeed. Lift up
sober toward truth a scared self-estimate.

9

Surprise me on some ordinary day
with a blessing gratuitous. Even I've done good
beyond their expectations. What count we then
upon Your bounty?

Interminable: an old theologian
asserts that even to say You exist is misleading.
Uh-huh. I buy that Second-century fellow.
I press his withered glorifying hand.

You certainly do not as I exist,
impersonating as well the meteorite
& flaring in your sun your waterfall
or blind in caves pallid fishes.

Bear in mind me, Who have forgotten nothing,
& Who continues. I may not foreknow
& fail much to remember. You sustain
imperial desuetudes, at the kerb a widow.

10

Fearful I peer upon the mountain path
where once Your shadow passed, Limner of the clouds
up their phantastic guesses. I am afraid,
I never until now confessed.

I fell back in love with you, Father, for two reasons:
You were good to me, & a delicious author,
rational & passionate. Come on me again,
as twice you came to Azarias & Misael.

President of the brethren, our mild assemblies
inspire, & bother the priest not to be dull;
keep us week-long in order; love my children,
my mother far & ill, far brother, my spouse.

Oil all my turbulence as at Thy dictation
I sweat out my wayward works.
Father Hopkins said the only true literary critic is Christ.
Let me lie down exhausted, content with that.

11

Germanicus leapt upon the wild lion in Smyrna,
wishing to pass quickly from a lawless life.
The crowd shook the stadium.
The proconsul marvelled.

'Eighty & six years have I been his servant,
and he has done me no harm.
How can I blaspheme my King who saved me?'
Polycarp, John's pupil, facing the fire.

Make too me acceptable at the end of time
in my degree, which then Thou wilt award.
Cancer, senility, mania,
I pray I may be ready with my witness.

FROM

Delusions, Etc.

(1972)

Opus Dei

(a layman's winter mockup, wherein moreover
the Offices are not within one day said
but thro' their hours at intervals
over many weeks—such being the World)

> *Lord, have mercy on my son: for he is lunatick,*
> *and sore vexed: for ofttimes he falleth into*
> *the fire, and oft into the water.*

> *And he did evil, because he prepared not*
> *his heart to seek the Lord.*

LAUDS

Let us rejoice on our cots, for His nocturnal miracles
antique outside the Local Group & within it
& within our hearts in it, and for quotidian miracles
parsecs-off yielding to the Hale reflector.

Oh He is potent in the corners. Men
with Him are potent: quasars we intuit,
and sequent to sufficient discipline
we perceive this glow keeping His winter out.

My marvellous black new brim-rolled felt is both stuffy & raffish,
I hit my summit with it, in firelight.
Maybe I only got a Yuletide tie
(increasing sixty) & some writing-paper

but ha (ha*ha*) I've bought myself a hat!
Plus-strokes from position zero! Its feathers sprout.
Thank you, Your Benevolence!
permissive, smiling on   our silliness You forged.

MATINS

Thou hard. I will be blunt: Like widening
blossoms again glad toward Your soothe of sun
& solar drawing forth, I find meself
little this bitter morning, Lord, tonight.

Less were you tranquil to me in my dark
just now than tyrannous. O some bore down
sore with enticements—One abandoned me—
half I swelled up toward—till I crash awake.

However, lo, across what wilderness
in vincible ignorance past forty years
lost to (as now I see) Your sorrowing
I strayed abhorrent, blazing with my Self.

I thought I was in private with the Devil
hounding me upon Daddy's cowardice
(trustless in stir the freeze: 'Do your own time').
Intertangled all—choking, groping bodies.

'Behold, thou art taken in thy mischief,
because thou art a bloody man' with horror
loud down from Heaven did I not then hear,
but sudden' was received,—appointed even

poor scotographer, far here from Court,
humming over goodnatured Handel's Te Deum.
I waxed, upon surrender, strenuous
ah almost able service to devise.

I am like your sun, Dear, in a state of shear—
parts of my surface are continually slipping past others,
not You, not You. O I may, even, wave
in crisis like a skew Wolf-Rayet star.

Seas and hills, the high lakes, Superior,
accomplish your blue or emerald donations—
manifest too your soft forbearance, hard
& flint for fierce man hardly to take in.

I take that in. Yes. Just now. I read that.

Hop foot to foot, hurl the white pillows about,
jubilant brothers: He is our overlord,
holding up yet with crimson flags the Sun
whom He'll embark soon mounting fluent day!

PRIME

Occludes wild dawn. Up thro' green ragged clouds
one sun is tearing, beset alders sway
weary under swollen sudden drops
and February winds shudder our doors,

Lord, as thou knowest. What fits me today
which work I can? I've to poor minimum
pared my commitments; still I'm sure to err
grievous & frequent before Evensong

and both I long toward & abhor that coming
Yet *if* You and I make a majority
(as old Claudel encouraged) what sharp law
can pass this morning?—upon which, I take heart.

Also: 'The specific gravity of iron
is one and one-half times the size of Switzerland.'
Zany enlivens. People, pipe with pipes:
the least of us is back on contract, even

unto myself succeeding in sunrise
all over again!
                    All customary blessings,
anathemas of the date (post-Lupercal,
and sure The Baby was my valentine),

I'm not Your beaver, here disabled, still
it is an honour, where some have achieved,

to limp behind along, humming, & keen
again upon what blue trumps, hazy, vainless glory.

In Alexandria, O Saint Julian
gouty, chair-borne, displayed then on a camel
thorough the insufferable city, and burned.
In other places, many other holy

bishops, confessors, and martyrs. Thanks be to God.

INTERSTITIAL OFFICE

Bitter upon conviction
(even of the seven women jurors
several wept) I will not kneel just now,
Father. I know I must

but being black & galled for these young men,
sick with their savage Judge
('we felt we had no alternative,
since all their evidence was ordered stricken')—

deep fatigue.
Conducting his own defence: 'men do pass laws
that usurp God's power . . .
I hope you'll try in your own way to speak peace.

God guide you.' Grim the prosecutor:
'He's trying to weasel his way out of it.'
Draft records here would have gone up in fire.
Peasant ladies & poupies there   went up go up in fire.

Who sat thro' all three trials tells me the juror in blue
looked inconsolably sad, and hid her eyes,
when one propped up on his table a little hand-lettered sign
WE LOVE YOU.

The judge is called P N.
This is of record. Where slept then Your lightning?
Loafed Your torque.
Well. Help us all! Yes—yes—I kneel.

TERCE

Oh half as fearful for the yawning day
where full the Enemy's paratus and
I clearly may
wholly from prime time fail, as yet from yesterday

with good heart grateful having gone no more
(under what gentle tempting You knew I bore)
than what occurred astray,
I almost at a loss now genuflect and pray:

Twice, thrice each day five weeks at 'as we forgive
those who trespass against us' I have thought
ah his envenomed & most insolent missive
and I have *done* it!—and I damn him still

odd times & unawares catch myself at it:
I'm not a good man, I won't ever be,
there's no health in here. You expect too much.
This pseudo-monk is all but at despair.

My blustering & whining & *ill* will
versus His will—Forgive my insolence,
since when I was a fervent child to You
and Father Boniface each 5 a.m.

But this world that was not. Lavender & oval,
lilac, dissolve into one's saying hurriedly
'In sex my husband is brutal, beating, dirty, and drunk.'
Has this become Thy will, Thou Reconciler?

I seem to hear Retreat blast thro' bleared air
back to an unassailable redoubt,
even old Nile-sounds, where 'tears' & 'men' sound the same
and 'not to be' & 'be complete' are one.

Ugh. What the *hell* quail I perplexed about?
Christ Jesus. Gethsemane & Calvary
& the Emmaus road, hardly propose
(someone was saying) most of us are lost.

SEXT

High noon has me pitchblack, so in hope out,
slipping thro' stasis, my heart skeps a beat
actuellement,
reflecting on the subtler menace of decline.

Who mentioned in his middle age 'Great Death
wars in us living which will have us all'
caused choreographers to tinker maps
pointing a new domestic capital

and put before Self-Preservation '1)'.
We do not know, deep now the dire age on,
if it's so, or mere a nightmare of one dark one,
Mani's by no means ultimate disciple.

I personally call it: outmoded biology,
of even mutation ignorant,
and in that, that a bare one in 100 is benevolent.

I wish You would clear this up. Moreover, I know
it may extend millennia, or ever, till
you tell somebody to. Meantime: Okay.
Now hear this programme for   my remnant of today.

Corpuscle-Donor, to the dizzy tune
of half a hundred thousand while I blink
losing that horrid same
scarlet amount and reel intact ahead:

so of rare Heart repair my fracturing heart
obedient to disobedience
minutely, wholesale, that come midnight neither
my mortal sin nor thought upon it lose me.

NONES

Problem. I cannot come among Your saints,
it's not in me—'Velle' eh?—I will, and fail.
But I would rather not be lost from You—
if I could hear of a middle ground, I'd opt:

a decent if minute salvation, sort of, on some fringe.
I am afraid, afraid. Brothers, who if
you are afraid are my brothers—veterans of fear—
pray with me now in the hour of our living.

It's Eleseus' grave makes the demons tremble,
I forget under what judge he conquered the world,
we're not alone here. Hearing Mark viii, though,
I'm sure to be ashamed of by. I am ashamed.

Riotous doubt assailed me on the stair,
I paused numb. Not much troubled with doubt,
not used to it. In a twinkling can man be lost?
Deep then in thought, and thought brought no relief.

But praying after, and somewhat after prayer
on no occasion fear had gone away!
I was alone with You again: 'the iron did swim.'
It has been proved to me again & again

He does *not* want me to be lost. Who does? The other.
But 'a man's shaliach is as it were himself':
I am Your person.

I have done this & that which I should do,
and given, and attended, and been still,
but why I do so I cannot be sure,
I am suspicious of myself. Help me!

I am olding & ignorant, and the work is great,
daylight is long, will ever I be done,
for the work is not for man, but the Lord God.
Now I have prepared with all my might for it

and mine O shrinks a micro-micro-minor
post-ministry, and of Thine own to Thee I have given,
and there is none abiding but woe or Heaven,
teste the pundits. Me I'm grounded for peace.

Flimsy between cloth, what may I attain
who slither in my garments? there's not enough of me,
Master, for virtue. I'm loose, at a loss.

Lo, where in this whirlpool sheltered in bone,
only less whirlpool bone, envisaging,
a sixtieth of an ounce to every pint,
sugar to blood, or coma or convulsion,

I hit a hundred and twenty notes a second
as many as I may to the glory of confronting—
unstable man, man torn by blast & gale—
Your figure, adamantly frontal.

VESPERS

Vanity! hog-vanity, ape-lust
slimed half my blue day, interspersed
solely almost with conversation feared,
difficult, dear, leaned forward toward & savoured,
survivaling between. I have not done well.
Contempt—if even the man be judged sincere—
verging on horror, top a proper portion,
of the poor man in paracme, greeding still.

That's nothing, nothing! For his great commands
have reached me here—to love my enemy
as I love me—which is quite out of the question!
and worse still, to love You *with my whole mind*—

insufferable & creative addition to Deuteronomy 6—

Shift! Shift!
            Frantic I cast about abroad
for avenues of out: Who really this this?
Can *all* be lost, then? (But some do these things . .
I flinch from some horrible saints half the happy mornings—

so that's blocked off.) Maybe it's not God's voice
only Christ's only. (But our Lord is our Lord.
No vent there.) If more's demanded of man than can
ma summon, You're unjust. Suppose not. See Jewish history,

tormented & redeemed, millennia later
in Freud & Einstein forcing us sorry & free,

Jerusalem Israeli! flames Anne Frank
a beacon to the Gentiles weltering.

With so great power bitter, so marvellous mild even mercy?
It's not conformable. It must be so,
but I am lost in it, dire Friend. Only I remember
of Solomon's cherubim 'their faces were inward.'

And thro' that veil of blue, & crimson, & linen,
& blue, You brood across forgiveness and
the house fills with a cloud, so that the priests
cannot stand to minister   by reason of the cloud.

COMPLINE

I would at this late hour as little as may be
(in-negligent Father) plead. Not that I'm not attending,
only I kneel here spelled
under a mystery of one midnight

un-numbing now toward sorting in & out
I've got to get as little as possible wrong
O like Josiah then I heard with horror
instructions ancient as for the prime time

I am the king's son who squat down in rags
declared unfit by wise friends to inherit
and nothing of me left but skull & feet
& bloody among their dogs the palms of my hands.

Adorns my crossbar Your high frenzied Son,
mute over catcalls. How to conduct myself?
Does 'l'affabilité, l'humilité'
drift hither from the Jesuit wilderness,

a programme so ambitious? I am ambitious
but I have always stood content with towers
& traffic quashing thro' my canyons wild,
gunfire & riot fan thro' new Detroit.

Lord, long the day done—lapse, & by bootstraps,
oaths & toads, tranquil microseconds,
memory engulphing, odor of bacon burning
again—phantasmagoria prolix—

a rapture, though, of the Kingdom here here now
in the heart of a child—not far, nor hard to come by,
but natural as water falling, cupped
& lapped & slaking the child's dusty thirst!

If He for me as I feel for my daughter,
being His son, I'll sweat no more tonight
but happy snore & drowse. I have got it made,
and so have all we of contrition, for

if He loves me He must love everybody
and Origen was right & Hell is empty
or will be at apocatastasis.
Sinners, sin on. We'll suffer now & later

but not forever, dear friends & brothers! Moreover:
my old Black freshman friend's mild formula
for the quarter-mile, 'I run the first 220
as fast as possible, to get out in front.

Then I run the second 220 even faster,
to stay out in front.' So may I run for You,
less laggard lately, less deluded man
of oxblood expectation
with fiery little resiny aftertastes.

Heard sapphire flutings. The winter will end. I remember You.
The sky was red. My pillow's cold & blanched.
There are no fair bells in this city. This fireless house
lies down at Your disposal as usual! Amen!

Tampa Stomp

The first signs of the death of the boom came in the summer,
early, and everything went like snow in the sun.
Out of their office windows. There was miasma,
a weight beyond enduring, the city reeked of failure.

The eerie, faraway scream of a Florida panther,
gu-roomp of a bull-frog. One broker we knew
drunk-driving down from Tarpon Springs flew free
when it spiralled over & was dead without one mark on him.

The Lord fled that forlorn peninsula
of fine sunlight and millions of fishes & moccasins
& Spanish moss & the Cuban bit my father
bedded & would abandon Mother for.

Ah, an antiquity, a chatter of ghosts.
Half the fish now in half the time
since those blue days died. We're running out
of time & fathers, sore, artless about it.

The Handshake, The Entrance

'You've got to cross that lonesome valley' and
'You've got to cross it by yourself.'
'Ain't no one gwine cross it for you,
You've got to cross it by yourself.'
Some say John was a baptist, some say John was a Jew,
some say John was just a natural man

addin' he's a preacher too?

'You've got to cross that lonesome valley,'
Friends & lovers, link you and depart.
This one is strictly for me.
I shod myself & said goodbye to Sally
Murmurs of other farewells half broke my heart
I set out sore indeed.

The High King failed to blossom on my enterprise.
Solely the wonderful sun shone down like lead.
Through the ridges I endured,
down in no simple valley I opened my eyes,
with my strong walk down in the vales & dealt with death.
I increased my stride, cured.

Henry's Understanding

He was reading late, at Richard's, down in Maine,
aged 32? Richard & Helen long in bed,
my good wife long in bed.
All I had to do was strip & get into my bed,
putting the marker in the book, & sleep,
& wake to a hot breakfast.

Off the coast was an island, P'tit Manaan,
the bluff from Richard's lawn was almost sheer.
A chill at four o'clock.
It only takes a few minutes to make a man.
A concentration upon now & here.
Suddenly, unlike Bach,

& horribly, unlike Bach, it occurred to me
that *one* night, instead of warm pajamas,
I'd take off all my clothes
& cross the damp cold lawn & down the bluff
into the terrible water & walk forever
under it out toward the island.

King David Dances

Aware to the dry throat of the wide hell in the world
O trampling empires, and mine one of them,
and mine one gross desire against His sight
slaughter devising there,
some good behind, ambiguous ahead,
revolted sons, a pierced son, bound to bear,
mid hypocrites amongst idolaters,
mockt in abysm by one shallow wife,
with the ponder both of priesthood & of State
heavy upon me, yea,
all the black same I dance my blue head off!

Henry's Fate & Other Poems, 1967–1972

(1977)

With arms outflung the clock announced: Ten-twenty.
Dozens of demons sprang & preyed on Henry.
All on a heavy morning.
The baby was ill, the sky was dark, the I
was Id, somebody put the sky on like a lid,
somebody who is not returning.

Oh we'll wait. After all, after all.
The Doubter & the rest. They rested all,
on the night of the crucifying.
Perhaps their dreams were something truly remarkable.
Perhaps their dreams had what to do with his dying—
but that was very lonely.

Haldol & Serax, phenobarbital,
Vivactil, by day; by deep night Tuinal
& Thorazine,
kept Henry going, like a natural man.
I'm waiting for them to work, as sometimes they can,
honey, in the bloodstream.

June 68

Good words & irreplaceable: serenade, schadenfreude,
angst & malheur, we need them, we bow to them:
what raving genius
in our past coined such wisdom? I cannot know.
Nor can you, my deep dear. You cannot know.
They were ineffable.

Who coined despair? I hope you never hear,
my lovely dear, of any such goddamned thing.
Set it up on a post
and ax the post down while the angels sing,
& bury the stenchful body loud & clear
with an appropriate toast.

Who made you up? That was a thin disguise:
the soul shows through. You are my honey dear.
Come, come & live with me.
I can deal with everything but your eyes
in tears—tears I invented & put there,
during our mystery.

24 June 68

I'm reading my book backward. It sounds odd.
It came twenty minutes ago. The hell with god.
A student just called up
about a grade earlier in the year.
The hell with students. And my mother ('Mir')
did the indexes to this book.

There's madness in the book. And sanenesses,
he argued. Ha! It's all a matter of
control (& so forth) of the subject.
The subject? Henry House & his troubles, yes
with his wife & mother & baby, yes
we're now at the end, enough.

A human personality, that's impossible.
The lines of nature & of will, that's impossible.
I give the whole thing up.
Only there resides a living voice
which if we can make we make it out of choice
not giving the whole thing up.

Phase Four

I will begin by mentioning the word
'Surrender'—that's the 4th & final phase.
The word. What is the thing, well, must be known
in Heaven. 'Acceptance' is the phase before;

if after finite struggle, infinite aid,
ever you come there, friend,
remember backward me lost in defiance,
as I remember those admitting & complying.

We cannot tell the truth, it's not in us.
That truth comes hard. O I am fighting it,
my Weapon One: I know I cannot win,
and half the war is lost, that's to say won.

The rest is for the blessed. The rest is bells
at sundown off across a dozen lawns,
a lake, two strands of laurel, where they come
out of phase three mild toward the sacristy.

Epilogue

(1942)

Epilogue

He died in December. He must descend
Somewhere, vague and cold, the spirit and seal,
The gift descend, and all that insight fail
Somewhere. Imagination one's one friend
Cannot see there. Both of us at the end.
Nouns, verbs do not exist for what I feel.

ACKNOWLEDGMENTS

INDEX OF FIRST LINES

INDEX OF TITLES

Acknowledgments

I would like to thank April Bernard, Henri Cole, Philip Coleman, Jonathan Galassi, David Godwin, John Haffenden, Michael Hofmann, Miranda Popkey, Charles Thornbury, and very especially Kate Donahue.

Index of First Lines

He died in December. He must descend   155
He was reading late, at Richard's, down in Maine,   144
High noon has me pitchblack, so in hope out,   134
Holy, & holy. The damned are said to say   115
Holy, as I suppose I dare to call you   112
Huffy Henry hid   the day,   75

I heard, could be, a Hey there from the wing,   84
I lift—lift you five States away your glass,   31
I put those things there.—See them burn.   17
I remind myself at that time of Plato's uterus—   103
I told him: The time has come, I must be gone.   10
I will begin by mentioning the word   152
I wished, all the mild days of middle March   27
I would at this late hour as little as may be   140
'If I had said out passions as they were,'   99
If I say Thy name, art Thou there? It may be so.   114
I'm cross with god who has wrecked this generation.   91
I'm reading my book backward. It sounds odd.   151
I'm scared a lonely. Never see my son,   82
In my serpentine researches   105
It seems to be DARK all the time.   109
It was the blue & plain ones. I forgot all that.   88
Itself a lightning-flash ripping the 'dark   34
I've found out why, that day, that suicide   29

Let us rejoice on our cots, for His nocturnal miracles   126
Life, friends, is boring. We must not say so.   79
Love her he doesn't but the thought he puts   85
Lover & child, a little sing.   67

Master of beauty, craftsman of the snowflake,   110
Misunderstanding. Misunderstanding, misunderstanding.   93
My daughter's heavier. Light leaves are flying.   96

Nothin very bad happen to me lately.   86

O when I grunted, over lines and her,   101
Occludes wild dawn. Up thro' green ragged clouds   129
Oh half as fearful for the yawning day   132
On the night of the Belgian surrender the moon rose   14

Problem. I cannot come among Your saints,   136

(. . rabid or dog-dull.) Let me tell you how   18

Sick with the lightning lay my sister-in-law,   20
Sole watchman of the flying stars, guard me   113
Surprise me on some ordinary day   119

—That's enough of that, Mr Bones. *Some* lady you make.   90
The animal moment, when he sorted out her tail   89
The first signs of the death of the boom came in the summer,   142
The glories of the world struck me, made me aria, once.   80
The Governor your husband lived so long   41
The grey girl who had not been singing stopped,   21
The history of strangers in their dreams   12
The round and smooth, my body in my bath,   16
The sun rushed up the sky; the taxi flew;   9
The three men coming down the winter hill   3
The weather was fine. They took away his teeth,   78
The women of Kilkenny weep when the team loses,   94
There sat down, once, a thing on Henry's heart   81
They may suppose, because I would not cloy your ear—   32
This afternoon, discomfortable dead   7
Thou hard. I will be blunt: Like widening   127

Under new management, Your Majesty: 116

Vanity! hog-vanity, ape-lust   138

What is the boy now, who has lost his ball, 6
Who am I worthless that You spent such pains 118
With arms outflung the clock announced: Ten-twenty. 149

You come blonde visiting through the black air 36
You should be gone in winter, that Nature mourn 33
Your shining—where?—rays my wide room with gold; 28
'You've got to cross that lonesome valley' and 143

Index of Titles